THE COMING OF THE LORD JESUS CHRIST

For the Lord Himself will descend from heaven with a shout, with the voice of an archangel, and with the trumpet of God. And the dead in Christ will rise first.
1 Thessalonians *4:16* (NJKV)

Therefore comfort one another with these words.
1 Thessalonians 4:18 *(NJKV)*

Bishop Everett H. Jefferson, Sr.

WESTBOW
PRESS®
A DIVISION OF THOMAS NELSON
& ZONDERVAN

WestBow Press books may be ordered through booksellers or by contacting:

WestBow Press
A Division of Thomas Nelson & Zondervan
1663 Liberty Drive
Bloomington, IN 47403
www.westbowpress.com
844-714-3454

Because of the dynamic nature of the Internet, any web addresses or links contained in this book may have changed since publication and may no longer be valid. The views expressed in this work are solely those of the author and do not necessarily reflect the views of the publisher, and the publisher hereby disclaims any responsibility for them.

Any people depicted in stock imagery provided by Getty Images are models, and such images are being used for illustrative purposes only. Certain stock imagery © Getty Images.

Editor: Jenese Tucker

Scripture quotations marked NIV are taken from the Holy Bible, New International Version®, NIV®. Copyright © 1973, 1978, 1984 by Biblica, Inc.™ Used by permission of Zondervan. All rights reserved worldwide.

Scripture quotations marked NKJV are taken from the New King James Version. Copyright © 1982 by Thomas Nelson, Inc. Used by permission. All rights reserved.

ISBN: 979-8-3850-0110-1 (sc)
ISBN: 979-8-3850-0111-8 (e)

Library of Congress Control Number: 2023911307

Print information available on the last page.

WestBow Press rev. date: 07/11/2023

The Coming of the Lord Jesus Christ

But I do not want you to be ignorant, brethren, concerning those who have fallen asleep, lest you sorrow as others who have no hope. 14 For if we believe that Jesus died and rose again, even so God will bring with Him those who sleep in Jesus. For this we say to you by the word of the Lord, that we who are alive and remain until the coming of the Lord will by no means precede those who are asleep. For the Lord Himself will descend from heaven with a shout, with the voice of an archangel, and with the trumpet of God. And the dead in Christ will rise first. Then we who are alive and remain shall be caught up together with them in the clouds to meet the Lord in the air. And thus we shall always be with the Lord. Therefore comfort one another with these words.
1 Thessalonians *4:13-18* (NKJV)

Dedication

I dedicate this book to my wife, Elaine Jefferson three sons and their wives, Everett Jefferson II and Dorsharica Jefferson, Eric and Dawn Jefferson, Elliot and Schnelle Jefferson. My ministerial colleagues. My grandsons and granddaughters have given me an abundance of ministerial support by the preaching and teaching of the Gospel, administrative, as well as musical help for the building of the Kingdom of God. I thank my wife, Elaine W. Jefferson for her committed effort in helping me with the promotion and sales of this book and others help that allow me to continue working on the charge the Lord has given me. My wife has given me her constant encouragement to express my God given thoughts through public speaking, writing, and publishing. Her God given motivation inspires me to keep writing even in my sickness and pain. I love Elaine and pray she will be with me throughout the time Almighty God gives us both on earth. I also dedicate this book to the memories of my mother, the late Katie Jefferson, and grandmother, the late Pearl

Juitt, schoolteachers who encouraged me to learn the necessary course work for my career in public speaking and writing. My father the late Percy Jefferson who encouraged me to do well in school and live according to the Laws of God. Other schoolteachers throughout my educational career that allowed me to be proficient in my educational studies, as I practice English, Language Arts, and other academic studies that would help me be efficient in my educational career. My educators also taught me to be efficient in communication skills that allowed me to be successful with my peers. I am grateful for the late Dr. Steven Haymon Ed. D, a professor of psychology who has written several books in his field and practiced psychology in the greater Saint Louis, Missouri area. The Professors of the Loyola University of Maryland provided me with the necessary skills to write and helped me to develop the art of expression through writing. My Biblical skills and knowledge were developed at the Bethesda Temple Church in St. Louis, Missouri, pastored by the late Bishop James A. Johnson. It is difficult to name all the people that had a great influence in my life. Many relatives, schoolteachers, friends, and co-workers have encouraged me to do great things and helped me to continue in my educational field. I have learned so much from so many people. I love and respect those who helped me achieve the wisdom and knowledge to express myself verbally and literally. I am grateful to acknowledge all that have given me wisdom to express God's Word and live in a domain that gives courage and strength to live what I teach and preach. I believe that expressing the good things in life and encouraging others to be good citizens of heaven and earth is part of our Godly commitment on earth. We should also be helpful to others, growing and developing in the good things that Almighty God desires for all of us to do. I will always be grateful for the help I have received throughout my spiritual and educational careers. I pray God's richest blessing upon all that have helped me to become the husband, minister, teacher, and friend that I am today.

Preface

The Coming of our Lord Jesus Christ, *(I Thessalonians 4:8-11)*. In this 21st century when we are informed about the coming of the Lord, we may become excited for a moment, but we soon shift back to our day-to-day activities. We soon forget that the Lord has informed us through His Word in *I Thessalonians 4:8-11*, that He would return and take His people out of the earth. We are instructed in *Revelation 3:14-22* that we are living in the last stages of the church. The Bible has informed us that the church would be neither cold nor hot but lukewarm. We are experiencing this as we see the body of Christ decrease in its excitement for the things of God. *Revelation 3:17* reveals a clear picture of where the church is today and in the future. Note what the Word of the Lord declares, *"Because you say, 'I am rich, have become wealthy, and have need of nothing'—and do not know that you are wretched, miserable, poor, blind, and naked—" (Revelation 3:17, NKJV).* It is obvious that the lukewarm nature has found its way into the 21st century church. We are blessed with some of the best living conditions ever, great modes of transportation, good jobs, and an abundance of food! Please do not misunderstand me. God is allowing us to be blessed with all these things. However, as we enjoy all these blessings, please do not forget our Lord Jesus Christ who came to earth, and willingly gave His life that we may have eternal life! Now is the time for the children of God to expect and prepare for the Lord's return. Consider the Word of the Lord. *"Now when He had spoken these things, while they watched, He was taken up, and a cloud received Him out of their sight. And while they looked steadfastly toward heaven as He went up, behold, two men stood by them in white apparel, who also said, "Men of Galilee, why do you stand gazing up into heaven? This same Jesus, who was taken up from you into heaven, will so come in like manner as you saw Him go into heaven." (Acts 1:9-11, NKJV).* The Apostle Paul reminds us that the Lord is coming back for His Church, His Body, His Bride. Do not forget that we are the church. We are His Body and at the coming of the Lord, we will soon become His Bride! Since we are in this church age and the church has become lukewarm; remove yourselves from being lukewarm and switch to the hot mode. In doing so you will see the glory of God and be ready for the coming of the Lord! Jesus declared, *"I stand at the door and knock..." (Revelation 3:20a, NKJV).*

Jesus is knocking on the door of each of our hearts. He wants each of us to come back to His designated place in our hearts and enjoy the sweet communion that we once shared with Him! There are so many things in this life that have distracted us from expecting the return of the Lord Jesus. Nevertheless, Jesus has given us the power to overcome whatever has pulled us away from Him. Note Jesus' declaration in the scripture: *"To him who overcomes I will grant to sit with Me on My throne, as I also overcame and sat down with My Father on His throne. "He who has an ear, let him hear what the Spirit says to the churches." (Revelation 3:21-22, NKJV).* The Lord has given us that overcoming power through the Holy Spirit that resides in us. The Holy Spirit that is dwelling in us will give us the power to overcome every wicked force that has moved us to that lukewarm state. Are you ready to overcome the lukewarm state and become hot again for the things of God? There is an old song that remains in my heart since I gave my life to the Lord Jesus Christ...

> *"Oh, I want to see Him, look upon His face,*
> *There to sing forever of His saving grace;*
> *On the streets of glory let me lift my voice,*
> *Cares all past, home at last, ever to rejoice."*

When I experience the evil forces in the earth and the devil's determination to make me turn away from God, I am even more determined to fight the good fight of faith and see the glory of the Lord working in my life. No, I do not want to go into hiding and give up on the Lord, but I will keep worshiping, fighting, and stay in love with Jesus Christ that I might be received when the Lord returns to receive His church. One of the old Gospel songs declared, *"I'm Gonna Work Until the Day Is Done."* Almighty God knows the day of His return to earth to receive His children, and I want to be ready when He comes! Since we do not know the day nor the hour of His return, it behooves us to be ready when Jesus comes and takes us into Heaven. I'm looking forward to that day and I am doing all that I can to make my calling and election a sure thing! What about you? The time is short, and it will not be long until the day the Lord Jesus returns to receive His bride! I want to be ready, how about you?

Contents

Introduction

Remember the Word of the Lord to the children of God, by the Apostle Paul, *"You are our epistle written in our hearts, known and read by all men; clearly you are an epistle of Christ, ministered by us, written not with ink but by the Spirit of the living God, not on tablets of stone but on tablets of flesh, that is, of the heart." (2 Corinthians 3:2-3, NKJV).* If Almighty God who has so graciously given us His Spirit, would He not also allow us to use the same Spirit in us to understand the things in our natural and spiritual lives? We do not need to be ignorant of anything. Almighty God has supplied us with His Spirit that gives us a wealth of knowledge and wisdom to help us overcome the world and the spiritual forces that try to overthrow and destroy us. I am convinced today that if any person lacks wisdom, the God of our salvation will freely give us wisdom because He is as close as the heart that beats within us, rather He lives within us. Just ask and you will receive the Spirit of the Living God that will live in you and prepare you to enter the Kingdom of

Heaven when the Lord Jesus returns to earth to receive His church!

It is no surprise to all of us that water is one of the most important substances in our natural lives. One of water's very important factors is the fact that is cleanses us from the daily accumulation of filth on our bodies. It is very important that we wash daily to cleanse and renew our skin for a healthy and glorious body. Therefore, we find it necessary to wash so that our natural skin is renewed and fresh for our benefit and for the benefit of others around us. It is interesting how natural wisdom can enlighten us spiritually. Just as the body needs to be washed and renewed so does our spirit! The Word of the Lord informs us: ***"...that He might sanctify and cleanse her with the washing of water by the word, that He might present her to Himself a glorious church, not having spot or wrinkle or any such thing, but that she should be holy and without blemish." (Ephesians 5:26-27, NKJV).***

We need the cleansing power of Almighty God's Word to wash away the spiritual filth that accumulates on our spirit. Just as our natural bodies are subject to get filthy so will our spirit. We are bombarded each day with filthy natural concepts and ideas that can accumulate in our spirit and affect the glory of Almighty God that wills to work in us. These spiritual concepts will spiritually illumine us and brighten our countenance. It is only the Word of the Lord that is able to cleanse us from the filth and renew our spirit, giving us the healthy look and feel that is so benefiting to us and to others that we associate with. No one wants to be around someone whose body has not been washed. This same principle will apply to those whose spirit is not clean. It is up to the believer to make sure that their spirit is washed and renewed every day by the Word of the Lord! When our bodies are washed and renewed, others will feel comfortable being around us. Likewise, when our spirit is washed and renewed, we attract others to us by the pleasant aroma of righteousness, joy, and peace that has been refreshed in our spirit by the cleansing of Almighty God's Word. I admonish all the saints of God to continue washing and renewing themselves by the Word of the Lord. When this is done, the glory of the Lord may emanate from your inner being and bless all that enter your space. When people see the glory of God in you, they may ask, *"what must I do to be like you, or rather what must I do to be saved."* Remember, the aroma of righteousness and peace that comes from the washing of the water by the Word will be a great blessing to everyone that meet you. It will motivate others to desire the same spiritual aroma that flows from your spirit!

Consider this scripture: ***"Do not be deceived, my beloved brethren. Every good gift and every perfect gift is from above, and comes down from the Father of lights, with whom there is no variation or shadow of turning." (James 1:16-17, NKJV).***

There is an old hymn that the members of the church would often sing many years ago entitled, *"Count Your Blessings Name Them One by One."* It continues with the words, *"Count your blessings see what God has done!"* This song is a reminder that God is the giver of good and perfect gifts, and the receiver of those gifts should take time to count, evaluate, and give thinks for what Almighty God has done. We are living in the last days as the Bible declares and we find that the days are evil and dangerous, and the people of this world are very unthankful. *(II Timothy 3:1-2, NKJV).* Even though the world may not exhibit its thankfulness to God and to each other, I do not feel that we should follow the ungodly character of the world. God has been too good to us that we do not give Him thanks.

All the wonderful gifts received in our natural life should be appreciated as we offer up to Almighty God the sacrifice of praise. Let's think about this for a moment... If we have good parents, children, and friends, it is a gift from God. Almighty God has surrounded us with people that love us, care for us, and are willing to do whatever it takes to make us happy. People that comfort us when we are sad, support us when we are weak, encourage us in times of despair, and bless us when life is financially unkind are good children of God. These are good gifts that come from above! The Word of the Lord also declares that Almighty God gives perfect gifts! Our salvation, which declares us righteous and free from sin and condemnation, is just the tip of the iceberg of the perfect gifts that Almighty God pours into our lives. God's perfect gifts removes us from the snare of the devil and from the pits of hell. Our perfect gifts give us eternal life with Jesus Christ and all the glory of the Kingdom of God. Our perfect gifts fill our souls with rivers of living water which spiritually and naturally enriches our lives.

Therefore, as I evaluate all the good and perfect gifts we have, I realize that I should have but one desire and purpose... *Give Thanks!* As often as I consider the great blessings from such gifts, I am eternally grateful, and I look for some way to elevate my praise to Almighty God. Lord I am so grateful for all the blessings that are in my life, all the things that have made me the spiritual and natural person that I am, and the glory that fills my life that I can see and feel. What a Mighty God we serve! Start evaluating your life today. Consider how good the Lord has been and give thanks with all your heart. I believe when we give thanks, God is pleased with our praise and will give us additional good and perfect gifts until He comes back to receive us into the Kingdom of God.

One

THE NEED FOR A SAVIOR/REDEEMER

When Adam fell from God's grace it had to be an awful and heartbroken condition for Almighty God. The very man He had formed out of the ground and breathed into his lungs the breath of life, has disobeyed His commandment, and fallen from grace. Adam's disobedience was not just to be glanced over and forgotten. It was a serious attack against the sovereignty of Almighty God. The Lord God made Adam perfect. Adam was created in the image of Almighty God and after His likeness. Adam had the ability and God given skills to name all the animals and other earthly things as he desired. Adam knew that it would break the heart of Almighty God if he would dishonor the Lord God by disobeying His Word. But Adam's heart was not focused on Almighty God but the helper that was given to him, a woman named Eve (the helper that was given to Adam was not named at that time). It is clearly stated that Adam's helper, Eve, was clearly deceived by the serpent. Adam was not deceived but clearly disobeyed by eating the forbidden fruit that he was strictly told not to eat. We cannot determine why Adam failed to obey Almighty God by eating the forbidden fruit and obey the desire of the woman that God gave him. We do know by the Word of the Lord, *"For as by one man's disobedience many were made sinners..." (Romans 5:19a, NKJV).* Almighty God made the perfect man but his imperfect movement to disobey Almighty God and obey the voice of his wife is what destroyed Adam and the entire world. Some may wrestle with the fact that Eve caused Adam to fall. The scripture clearly declares: *"For Adam was formed first, then Eve. And Adam was not deceived, but the woman being deceived, fell into transgression. (1 Timothy 2:13-14, NKJV).* Nevertheless, it was the disobedience of Adam that allowed sin to enter the world. Adam and Eve were removed from paradise (the Garden of Eden) and were not allowed to return. Even after Adam and Eve were expelled from the Garden of Eden, Almighty God made a promise of redemption for all mankind. *"So, the Lord God said to the serpent: "Because you have done this, You are cursed more than all cattle, And more than every beast of the field; On your belly you shall go, And you shall eat dust All the days of your life. And I will put enmity between you and the woman, And between your seed and her Seed;*

He shall bruise your head, And you shall bruise His heel." (Genesis 3:14-15, NKJV). The word enmity means to be actively opposed or hostile to someone or something. It is obvious as we examine the natural and spiritual conditions of this world, we are bombarded with opposition on every side. The Lord placed a curse on the serpent as He declared that the serpent would eat dust all his life. However, the ultimate curse on the serpent was that the Seed of the woman was going to bruise the serpent's head. Everything that the devil could think of to further hurt Almighty God's creation would be altered and destroyed but restored by the Seed of the woman.

It has become evident that the Seed of the woman would become our Lord Jesus Christ! Since the fall of Adam, man suffered the attacks of the devil and failed to remain steadfast with Almighty God and live. When we consider all that man has gone through since the fall of Adam, we find ourselves drowning in sin. Man's lack of faith and confidence to hold on to Almighty God's Word caused him to fall from grace. Even though sin had devastated the life of every child born into the world, the Lord God showed mercy to every generation by doing great and wonderful things to mankind and all the living creatures He had made. Even though sin had entered the world through Adam, the Lord had mercy on the man, woman, and their seed (offspring) that begin to multiply on the face of the earth. Almighty

God showed mercy to Adam and Eve by covering their nakedness with the fur of animals. These coats of skin were a much greater covering than the fig leaves that Adam and Eve first used. When Almighty God showed mercy on His human creation by covering them with the fur of an animal, it was one of the first, if not the first sacrifice of an animal for the sake of mankind.

It was evident that the Lord God loved the man and woman that He had made. Nevertheless, the man and his wife could no longer remain in the Garden of Eden, *(Genesis 3:23-24)*. Adam and Eve were expelled from the Garden of Eden and now having to suffer the task of toiling for food and other elements of life outside of the Garden of Eden. Adam had to work to provide the necessities of life and Eve would deal with the hardship of giving birth to children. It was evident that sin had entered the world as the first son Cain, got into an altercation with his brother Abel and killed him. When Almighty God inquired of Cain about Abel, he replied in a disrespectful way. The Lord God knew the disrespectful way Cain responded, and the way he presented his required sacrifice. Cain became a vagabond (a person who wanders from place to place without a fixed home) in the earth for the killing of his brother Abel, and his repulsive attitude towards Almighty God. Abel was considered a righteous son of God, yet he was killed by his brother Cain. Even in this day as we strive to live as righteous sons that are walking in the Spirit of

Almighty God. Nevertheless, the righteous are being persecuted by evil individuals that hate the movement of the Lord in the earth by His people. The unrighteous people are willing to do whatever they can to keep the righteous people from speaking the Word of the Lord or to do whatever is necessary to bring condemnation to their lives. Nevertheless, the Word of the Lord cannot be stopped, delayed, or altered by man. Remember when the king of Egypt heard that a deliverer for the children Israel was to be born, He made sure that all the male children were killed. Yes, many of the young children and babies of the Israelites were killed, but the one who was born to deliver the children of Israel from Egypt was spared. I marvel when I read the movements of the Lord God in the scriptures. The Lord will protect His children no matter what the enemy tries to do to destroy them! When I read these stories of faith I am motived and moved with expectation that the Lord God can and will do whatever He desires to protect His children from the devil. It gives me access to faith that motivates me to believe great things and opens my heart to be assured that the Word of the Lord given to His children will come to pass.

Adam and Eve had another child (Seth) replacing the murder of Abel. The earth grew more violent as the people on earth fought against each other over their likes and dislikes. However, there is one thing worth noting, several generations from Adam and Eve's first children, was a child born into this world by the name of Enoch, the father of Methuselah. This man lived the longest of all human beings. The scripture declares: ***"Enoch walked faithfully with God; then he was no more, because God took him away." (Genesis 5:24, NIV).*** This action by Almighty God (taking a live natural individual from earth to heaven) is only recorded twice in the Bible. The other individual was Elijah a prophet. What is this story saying to us today and how do we decipher its meaning for our lives? The key phrase in this scripture is, ***"Enoch walked with God."*** I believe Enoch possessed all the spiritual qualities that God was looking for in the human beings He created. I believe the greatest quality that Enoch possessed was *walking with God*; and considering all the great spiritual things the Lord God desired in man. I believe that walking with and pleasing God was a rare quality during this time. After the murder of Abel, sin and unrighteous acts became frequent on the earth. After Enoch was taken, (he did not see death) several generations after Noah were born. The wickedness on the earth was growing. Consider these scriptures: ***"Then the Lord saw that the wickedness of man was great in the earth, and that every intent of the thoughts of his heart was only evil continually. And the Lord was sorry that He had made man on the earth, and He was grieved in His heart." (Genesis 6:5-6, NKJV).*** Man declared himself independent of the rule of Almighty

God over mankind. Man was expelled from the Garden of Eden and had to suffer the hardships of working to provide for himself and family. Man could have shown gratitude towards Almighty God for the mercy the Lord God showed him. Instead of man trying to please the Lord and atone for his sins, he only got worse with his ungodly actions.

The Lord God repented that He had made man because of man's wickedness; and decided He would destroy all mankind. The Scriptures declare, ***"Noah found grace in the eyes of the Lord." (Genesis 6:8, NKJV).*** Almighty God had determined Noah to be a just man and even though there was violence and corruption in the earth, Noah and his family would be saved from the destruction that the Lord God would bring upon the earth. Noah's job was to build an ark that would cover his family and a specific amount of the clean and unclean animals on the earth. The Lord God determined that He would allow it to rain forty days and forty nights. The water would come from the sky as well as below the ground. This was Almighty God's judgment on the wicked people on the earth. Noah, his family, and all the animals he was instructed to bring in the ark would be saved from the flood. The complete story of Noah and his descendants is found in ***(Genesis Chapters 6-10).*** After the flood the earth had a new beginning. The Lord God placed a bow in the sky as a covenant between Himself and man that He would not destroy the earth by water again. However, there was not a significant change in the nature of mankind.

The significant change that took place on earth and before the Lord God, was the birth of Abram and Sarai. The Lord God makes a promise to Abram that he would be blessed. This is the summary of the promise: *"And in you all the families of the earth shall be blessed." (Genesis 12:3b, NKJV).* If we carefully read the life of Abram and his wife Sarai, his and her names were changed to Abraham and Sarah. We find that this was the beginning of a life and spirituality that changed the events on the earth. The spirituality of Abraham grew as his son Isaac was born. Other descendants were born through the seed of Abraham that allowed the spiritual legacy of Abraham to become a great nation that represents the sovereignty of Almighty God. The knowledge of Almighty God became known in the earth and continue to grow through the family of Abraham. The thing that set Abraham apart from the rest of the people in the world was his faith in Almighty God. The faith that was in the heart of Abraham allowed the Lord to consider him to be righteous. Since the beginning was stated in *(Genesis 1)*, there were only a few people declared righteous: Abel, Seth, Enoch, and Enosh were on the earth, and men begin to call on the Name of the Lord. However, as people increased on the earth wickedness also increased. The Lord God made the adjustments through dealing with the wickedness by raising up people that were able to exhibit godly influence in the earth that changed some of the people's ungodly nature. Nevertheless, the Lord God had a specific plan after the flood. Faith was the key element that would change the lives of people and give them a new start in living a righteous life before the Lord God. Abraham was moved by Almighty God to be obedient to the Word that was given to him. Please note the act of faith was started in the heart of Noah and significantly manifested in the heart of Abraham. Abraham's faith grew through his time and during the giving of the Mosaic Law to Moses. Faith continues to manifest through the Mosaic Law until grace entered through our Lord Jesus Christ. Now faith is the cornerstone of Christianity as we reference our faith in the Lord Jesus Christ! Faith is extremely impor in our lives. The Word of the Lord declares: ***"But without faith it is impossible to please Him, for he who comes to God must believe that He is, and that He is a rewarder of those who diligently seek Him." (Hebrews 11:6, NKJV).*** It is important that we believe every Word that the Lord God is speaking to us. When we hear the voice of the Lord speaking to us it is very important that we listen carefully and act on the Word that we hear. The action that we take is believing! Consider the scripture again: ***For what does the Scripture say? "Abraham believed God, and it was accounted to him for righteousness." (Romans 4:3, NKJV).*** When

9

the Lord speaks to us and we believe, and we act on Word, the Lord God declares us to be righteous. God tested Abraham when He told him to take his only son Isaac and offer him as a burnt offering on a mountain in the land of Moriah. Abraham did as the Lord told him by binding Isaac as the sacrifice and raising his knife to take his life. When the knife was raised the Lord God called out to Abraham telling him not to take Isaac's life. A ram was caught in the thicket by his horns. Abraham took his son Isaac from the altar and offered the ram that was caught in the thicket.

The word, trust or belief is used in the scriptures before the accrual word faith is used. The scriptures declare Abraham as the father of all that believed. *(Romans 4:11-12, 16).* Considered what the scriptures declared which started in Abraham's day until our time. Abraham's belief in God was determined as righteousness. *(Romans 4:3; Galatians 3:6; and James 2:23).* The righteousness of our faith begins with our belief. It is imperative that we believe Almighty God first, and our righteousness is declared by our movement by the Word given by Almighty God. The Lord God will not show us everything before it happens, but He will express to us by His Word and the outcome of what He has prepared for us. The true child of God is to believe and move in the direction the Lord God has spoken, completely trusting the Word He has given. If we study the Word of the Lord, we will find that many of the patriarchs were not completely aware of the next turn of events in their walk with the Lord. Nevertheless, the reward of their faith in God was evident as the promise that was made by the Word that was spoken by Almighty Lord. As humans we often wrestle with what Almighty God has spoken for us to do because we cannot see or understand how it is going to happen. However, the Lord Jesus reminded His followers to; *"Have faith in God."* When we walk with God, faith is not an option but a necessary criterion as we walk with Him to develop our walk and perfection in the Spirit. As we go through this book, we will understand the importance of walking with God and having the uttermost belief in the spoken and written Word that our faith be built up allowing nothing to destroy us spiritually. Remember, our faith in the Lord's return must be at its peak because the enemy will continually focus to get us to disbelieve what the Lord God has spoken. We will not give up on the Word of the Lord. Therefore, let us be confident that the Lord will return and keep His promise to His people.

Two

DEVELOPMENT OF A SAVIOR— ABRAHAM TO JACOB

Abraham, Sarah, Isaac, and Jacob (Israel) became the basic of faith in mankind as given by Almighty God. Faith in Almighty God grew in mankind as men and women believed and walked in the grace of our Lord God. Abraham was a type of Christ in that he was the prototypical stranger and foreigner. Like the Redeemer, He functionally *"had nowhere to lay his head."* As the federal head of the Covenant, he was also the father of many nations. Jesus is the *"Everlasting Father" (Isaiah 8:18, 9:6; Psalm 45:16; Hebrews 2:13),* of believers who federally represented His people from every tribe, nation, and language. The promises in Scripture are said to have been made to *"Abraham and his Seed... who is Christ."* All the promises made to Abraham were made to Him as the typical representative of the Covenant of Grace. Ultimately, they were made to, and fulfilled in Jesus Christ. Abraham is considered the father of faith. He believed God and it was accounted unto him for righteousness. *(Genesis 15:6; Romans 4:3; Galatians 3:6; and James 2:23).* The Lord God directed Abraham to leave the land where he lived and go to a place where the Lord was directing him. Have you ever thought about such a circumstance as this, going somewhere without a complete understanding of where you are going? It is obvious that Abraham was directed by Almighty God because the outcome of his movement was the successful gift of God. How many of us have considered the actions of Abraham and how it could be applied to our own life? Remember, Abraham heard the Lord God speak to him even while he was among people that were unbelievers. The scriptures declare that Abraham believed God, and because of his belief he was declared righteous. Abraham's belief in Almighty God allowed him to follow the path of righteousness that the Lord was giving him. When we read the story of Abraham and other heroes of faith, we find that they were tuned in to the voice of Almighty God. Therefore, when they heard the Lord speak, they reacted in a positive way that pleased the Lord. The reward of Almighty God was upon their lives because they believed and reacted to the Word that was given by the Lord God. Many times, the Word given did not immediately come to pass, but it was sure and effective as the Lord God had promised.

One of the greatest acts of faith in the life of Abraham

and Sarah was the promise of a son in their old age. Consider what God Almighty promised when Abraham was near one hundred years old, and Sarah was ninety years of age. Unbelievable and impossible, or this cannot happen many would say! Yet what the Lord God declared came to pass. As explained in chapter one, after the child was born and grew up as a young man, Abraham was tested. Almighty God informed Abraham to go to the land of Moriah, and offer Isaac, his only son Isaac, as a burnt offering. *(Genesis 22:2).* Abraham passed the test given by Almighty God by taking his son Isaac into the land of Moriah saying to Isaac when he asked about the lamb for the offering. Abraham replied to Isaac; *"My son, God will provide for Himself the lamb for a burnt offering." (Genesis 22:8, NKJV).* The Lord did provide Himself a lamb for the burnt offering just as He declared. The story continues as we understand that the Lord God comes in the person of Jesus Christ as the Sacrificial Lamb that would take away the sins of the world. Many of us that have given our lives to Christ understand that we have been redeemed by the Blood of our Lord Jesus Christ. Through this sacrificial process we are delivered from sin and waiting for the ultimate Messianic promise of the Lord God Almighty, the coming of the Lord Jesus! The Lord Jesus (Almighty God) provided for Himself the Lamb that would take away the sins of the world. Jesus rose from the dead and we (the church) are waiting for His return to take us into the Kingdom of God! Stated previously, Abraham is the person Almighty God chose to be the father of many nations. *(Genesis 17:4-5 and Romans 4:17-18)*. When men failed Almighty God in their spiritual walk, the Lord God selected someone He could rely on to continue the work of salvation to redeem mankind from sin. The Lord God chose Noah to do a specific work for the redemption of the earth after mankind and the whole earth was destroyed. However, mankind became spiritually corrupt again and disappointed the heart of Almighty God.

Mankind's confidence grew stronger in the Lord God until the nature of man outgrew the spiritual aspects given by God and violence again increased on the earth. The sons of (Israel) Jacob were an example of the spiritual decline of the spiritual nature of God's chosen. Jacob had twelve sons and one daughter. These twelve sons became the spiritual basis of the foundation of the children of Israel. Nevertheless, only two of the twelve sons (Judah and Joseph) were considered spiritually special before the Lord God. Judah means praise and Joseph was the survivor who became second in command in Egypt during the crucial times of the famine. The other sons had basic troublesome issues that were manifested against Joseph because of the dreams Almighty God had given him. Joseph became the son of Jacob's family that did what the Lord God commanded him which allowed his family to survive.

Throughout the Bible we can find many situations that rose up against family members and friends that would separate themselves from others because of their faith in Almighty God. Joseph knew when his brothers came to Egypt to get grain in order to survive. Joseph realized his purpose to save his family was divinely inspired by the Lord God. He knew that the bad things that his brothers did to him was for a greater purpose. Joseph forgave them and became a great blessing to his family. Throughout Biblical history we find that people in the world did awful things to others but by the grace of Almighty God these people had the mind of God to forgive them and yet bless them. Some Biblical references would declare Joseph as a type of Christ. Joseph was extremely mistreated by his brothers, yet he forgave them and blessed them without any adverse actions for their sinful behavior towards him. Joseph is considered a type of Jesus Christ, for his life was a type of sacrifice to save the lives of all Israel. Joseph was extremely mistreated by his brothers but, he forgave them and saved their lives by the abundant of food supplies he gave them during the time of a serious famine. Even though Joseph was mistreated by his brothers he forgave them and showed them the brotherly love that was necessary to save and sustain their lives. When we read the story of Joseph, we can clearly see that he is a type of Christ. He was mistreated by his brothers as they even left him in a pit to die. However, no matter how bad he was treated by his family, when his family was suffering from the famine, he had compassion on them and saved their lives.

Man's sinful actions towards each other and their disobedience towards Almighty God continued throughout time. Man disregarded the Word of the Lord and found himself out of the will of God. The Lord God continued to speak to His people as He spoke through Abraham and others but most of them declined to adhere to the Word of the Lord God. Unfortunately, the actions of most people were based on their own feeling, totally disregarding the Word of the Lord. The Lord God did not cast mankind aside because of their sinful actions. Consider Jacob, whose name means *supplanter* or *trickster*. Jacob did many things that conformed to the meaning of his name, yet the Lord dealt with him and changed his name to Israel, meaning, *a prince with God*! When we read about other children of God and their success in the Lord, we realize that a great change took place in their lives that brought them close to Almighty God and gave them spiritual purpose. The change that occurred in these children of God not only gave them great spiritual purpose but also caused others to change spiritually and enhance the lives of others. Throughout each generation the spiritual advancement of mankind increased. There were times that the spiritual advancement of mankind decreased yet because of the love and mercy of Almighty God, mankind rose to the spiritual occasion, repented, and gave themselves back to the Lord. Even during our lives in this twenty-first century, the same spiritual things may have happen causing us to fall from the grace of Almighty God. Nevertheless, the Lord has mercy on us and forgives us that we may not be eternally lost. Thank God for His wonderful grace and mercy that keeps us spiritually alive and well. Let us not give up and consider that all is lost when we fail. The Word of the Lord declares: *For He Himself has said, "I will never leave you nor forsake you." (Hebrews 13:5b, NKJV).* Therefore, throughout time the Lord God developed men and women to carry on the spiritual work necessary to prepare souls for the Kingdom of God. Almighty God is using all of us that are willing to be used to enhance His Kingdom. Do not be ashamed or fearful to do the work that the Lord is calling you to do. The Lord is with us, and He will give us the power and strength to complete the desired spiritual work He has ordained for our lives.

Three

MOSES THE SPIRITUAL DELIVERER FOR ISRAEL

Years after Joseph's leadership in Egypt there arose a ruler in Egypt that did not know Joseph and all the great things, he did to be a blessing to Egypt. The children of Israel began to multiply in Egypt and the new ruler of Egypt began to make things difficult for the children of Israel. The Israelites were enslaved about four hundred years and made to build up the Egyptian kingdom. During this time the children of Israel cried out to Almighty God because of their taskmasters. The Lord heard their cry and raised up a leader that would deliver them from this awful act of slavery. When the children of Israel began to multiply and become strong, Pharoah decided to have all male Israelite children killed. When Jochebed (Moses' mother) saw that the child was beautiful she hid the child for three months. But when she could no longer hide the child, she placed baby Moses in an ark that would float in the river.

Jochebed's daughter, Miriam, watched Moses float down the river to see what would happen to him. The baby Moses was retreated from the river by the servants of Pharaoh's daughter. Pharaoh's daughter named him Moses because he was drawn out of the water. When Moses grew up, he saw an Egyptian beating a Hebrew, one of his brethren. Moses killed the Egyptian and buried him in the sand. The next day Moses noticed two Hebrew men fighting among themselves. Moses chastised the one that was wrong. But the one that was wrong confronted Moses about killing the Egyptian and asked him would he do likewise to him. Moses left Egypt and went into the land of Midian. Soon thereafter the Lord called Moses, speaking to him through a bush that was burning but not consumed. Moses' instructions were to go back to the land of Egypt and deliver the children of Israel out of bondage. Moses is considered a type of Christ because he answered the call of Almighty God to deliver the children of Israel out of Egyptian bondage.

There are many types and shadows of Christ in the Old Testament. However, the more significant ones are the human beings that became deliverers for the people of Almighty God. Nevertheless, when things do not go as we think, doubts, fears, and some panic behavior become a part of our thinking and these adverse conditions affect the lives of the people of God. Likewise, we may turn away from what the Lord called us to do because of the difficulty of the task that the Lord is requiring us to do. Consider the scripture: ***"So Moses returned to the Lord and said, "Lord, why have You brought trouble on this people? Why is it You have sent me? For since I came to Pharaoh to speak in Your name, he has done evil to this people; neither have You delivered Your people at all." (Exodus 5:22-23, NKJV)***. Moses was concerned that the children of Israel were not being let go as Almighty God had promised. Many times, in our lives we may become disappointed when things do not come to pass as we expect. However, after the ten plagues the Word of the Lord was fulfilled as promised. The children of Israel were delivered from Egypt, and they were released from bondage just as the Lord promised. Moses led a significant number of people out of the land of Egypt. Through Moses many miracles were performed as the glory of Almighty God was active in Israel's life. One of the highlights of Moses leadership was Almighty God allowing the children of Israel crossing through the Red Sea on dry ground, and the giving of the Mosaic Law at Mount Sinai. One of the things we can be assured of is when Almighty God makes a promise, He will make sure that promise comes to pass! Our job is to believe what the Lord has said and patiently wait until God's promise is fulfilled. Throughout the scriptures we are informed that what the Lord God has said and the promised He has made to His people will come to pass. It is important that we wait with great expectation until the Lord God fulfills what He has promised. We have heard the expressions many times that the Lord cannot lie *(Titus 1:2)*. After many years of salvation, I believe what the Lord has spoken, and I will wait with great expectation on the promises that were given by the Lord.

Moses was a type of Christ, as indicated earlier. He was the deliverer and shepherd of many people. Moses sacrificed his time and resources to ensure that the people of God were blessed and care for as Almighty God instructed. Nevertheless, he was only a man that when human passions were evolved that causes him to become angered; he failed God and the people by being disobedient. One example of his human failure was when the Lord told him to speak to the rock and water would come out of it. *(Numbers 20:8)*. Moses was upset with the people and did not speak to the rock as the Lord God informed him, but smote the rock as the first time in disgust of the actions of the people. Moses' actions caused him the blessing of entering the Promise Land. Our actions before Almighty God should not be considered lightly. The Lord God means what He says and says what He means. There are many people in this world that consider being a pastor or a spiritual leader of people in this world. I would consider the cost and make certain that the Lord has made you His choice before entering any form of ministry that directly involves the lives of people. The people that the Lord calls into His kingdom are precious and to be cared for with love and gentleness. We cannot treat the people of Almighty God any way we humanly desire. Our treatment of Almighty God's people is to be with patience and love. The fruit of the spirit must be ingrained in the spiritual leader and manifested in the children of God that follow. The Lord God filled us with His Spirit that we may treat one another with the love and compassion the same way He has treated us. There are many spiritual leaders that feel they can treat the children of God any way they please. However, I beg to differ. The Lord God made choice of us because of His love for us. We know ourselves that if we really love our natural children, will we allow someone to mistreat them? I think not! Everything we do in Christianity should be an example of the love of Christ. Therefore, let us treat each other as the Lord is treating us and we will see the glory of the Lord in our lives.

When we read through the scriptures, we will find many types of Christs that point to our Lord and Savior Jesus Christ coming to earth and giving His life on a cross for the remission of our sins. The examples we find in the Bible before Christ gave His life and rose from the dead, were examples of what was to come for the redemption of mankind. The Pentateuch (Genesis • Exodus • Leviticus • Numbers • Deuteronomy) is the first five books of the Bible, also called the "Torah" in the Hebrew Scriptures and referred to the Books that Moses wrote. Though we often call these books "The Law," it is also called "The Torah" which does not mean "law," but "teaching." Basic to the Torah is the idea of the covenant. A covenant is an agreement. In the Bible the covenants are special because God is one of the parties to the covenant. Biblical covenants have three parts: a statement about God's saving act (what God brings to the agreement); a statement about what God expects from humanity in response; and a sign or symbol as a reminder of the covenant. As we read the Pentateuch, we will find many types and shadows of Jesus Christ. These types point to the birth, death, and resurrection of our Lord Jesus Christ. As mentioned before, there offerings were not perfect, sacrificial being such as animal sacrifices available on the earth that could atone for the sins of human beings. There were great men and women that could have given their lives for the sake of all mankind. However, none would have been the perfect sacrifice that would have pleased the Heart of Almighty God. Remember the scripture? *"But God demonstrates His own love toward us, in that while we were still sinners, Christ died for us. Much more then, having now been justified by His blood, we shall be saved from wrath through Him. (Romans 5:8-9, NKJV).* There is no justification from sin through human sacrifices. Only through the Blood of Jesus Christ are we justified from all unrighteousness and cleansed from all sin. Each of the sacrifices in the

Old Testament were types and shadows of things to come. Moses was instructed by the Lord God to build the Tabernacle and everything that it consisted, from the outer court to the Most Holy Place, to be the place when sacrifices were made and offered to cleanse the people from their sins. Nevertheless, these sacrifices were only temporary and could not permanently eradicate sin. Consider these scriptures: *"For the law, having a shadow of the good things to come, and not the very image of the things, can never with these same sacrifices, which they offer continually year by year, make those who approach perfect. For then would they not have ceased to be offered? For the worshipers, once purified, would have had no more consciousness of sins. But in those sacrifices, there is a reminder of sins every year. For it is not possible that the blood of bulls and goats could take away sins. (Hebrews 10:1-4, NKJV).* It was only through the Blood of Jesus Christ that we are made perfect. As the scripture mentions, the blood of bulls and goats could not take away sins; only the Blood of our Lord Jesus Christ can cleanse us from all sin that we may be presented perfect before Almighty God! The scriptures have indicated that the law is only a shadow of good things to come. The good thing that has come is Jesus Christ our Lord! Jesus' sacrifice at Calvary completed the work that man could not do. We have the right to the Tree of Life because of Jesus' sacrifice!

Four

JOSHUA (HOSHEA IS SALVATION) A SAVIOR

Joshua was a faithful assistant to Moses. Moses was instructed by Almighty God that he would not go into the Promised Land because he smote the rock instead of speaking to the rock as instructed. The Lord chose Joshua to lead the children of Israel out of the wilderness into the Promised Land. Joshua was a type of Christ as he was determined by the counsel of Almighty God to lead the children of Israel into the Promise Land. The Lord was with Joshua and gave him the military might to conqueror the enemies he would come up against. The Lord God spoke to Joshua these words: *"No man shall be able to stand before you all the days of your life; as I was with Moses, so I will be with you. I will not leave you nor forsake you." (Joshua 1:5, NJKV)*. When the children of Israel left the wilderness their first obstacle was the city of Jericho. Jericho was a city fortified with walls and gates that made it impossible to come in or leave out. However, the Word of the Lord came to Joshua with instructions as how to defeat each city that the Lord told him to enter into. Joshua's success was based on his relationship with Almighty God and his attention to the details that the Lord God had given him. I am always amazed by the Word of the Lord that comes into the lives of His people and my own life. The Lord cannot lie, and He always does things with a specific purpose. When we consider that the Lord is with us and that He will never leave us nor forsake us, how can we fail! Before Joshua entered his first land of conquest (Jericho), the Lord showed Himself to Joshua and gave him instructions as to how he would cross the Jordon and win each battle on the other side of the Jordon. It is important as children of God that we listen carefully to the Word of the Lord and respond appropriately. There are many battles we will encounter as we walk with Almighty God. Like Joshua we pay attention to the Word that the Lord is speaking to us. The Word that Joshua heard from the Lord directed all that were under his command to hear and respond accordingly as it was given. Joshua knew that a great battle was coming up and it was necessary for all to be on board as the Lord God had commanded to win the battles. It is important that we understand the will of the Lord for us to win the spiritual battles that come up against us. Remember, we do not fight alone but the Lord is with us, and we will exceed the expectations when the Lord shows us what to do in each battle. The victories that we win over our enemies will be an everlasting memory of the greatness of Almighty God!

It is imperative that we respond to the Word of the Lord and to spiritual leadership to experience the successful blessings in our walk in Christ. The most important things that I have experienced in my walk in Christ is understanding the written Word and submitting my life to Christ as much as possible. When we read the story of Joshua, we can clearly understand the reason that the Lord was with him. When Joshua was under the leadership of Moses there was no resistance from Joshua against Moses. Joshua also followed the instructions of the Lord God when he was placed in the leadership position that was given to Him by the Lord. Joshua also heard the Word of the Lord that declared he should be strong and very courageous! This was not a time to be afraid and withdrawn because of the power of the enemies surrounding him. However, like Joshua its time for ever warrior in Christ to be the powerful soldier that the Lord God has called us to be. *Joshua 5:13-15* expresses the boldness and courage of Joshua. He comes face to face with a Man that has His sword drawn. Joshua questions the Man asking him: *"Are You for us or for our adversaries?" So, He said, "No, but as Commander of the army of the Lord." (Joshua 5:13b-14a, NKJV).* When the Man identified Himself, Joshua bowed down and worshiped. This was a confirmation that the Lord God was with Joshua, and it was time to prepare for war and win! I believe the Lord does not give us instructions just to toss them aside and do what we wish. But it is imperative that we follow the directions we have been given by the Lord. With each conquest Joshua followed the instructions of the Lord and won! When the two men of God in Joshua's army came to Rahab's house to receive intel, they received it and gave Rahab and her family the assurance that they would be spared from the attacks of the enemy. I believe it is very important that when we receive instructions from the Lord God, we should follow such instructions with all our heart that those who have received the promise of God from us will believe and expect to see the glory of Almighty God in their lives. Just as Joshua was dedicated to do the will of Almighty God, we should also be dedicated to follow the commands of our Lord and be diligent to carry out the plans that the Lord God is requiring us to us do. In carrying out the plans of Almighty God in our daily walk, we will be spiritual successful, and the glory of God's presence will always be with us.

There was not one time found in the scriptures, that Joshua rebelled against the Lord and came up short of the promises of Almighty God. One of the remarkable characters of Joshua was his commitment to his leader, Moses and after taking over his commitment to the Lord God and Israel. There are no incidents when Joshua rebelled against God or led the people into a negative situation. One of the greatest positions of Joshua as a leader was the ability to stay focused and committed to the instructions that the Lord had given him. The Lord spoke to Joshua saying, *"I will not leave you nor forsake you." (Joshua 1:5b, NKJV).* This is a powerful word of faith spoken into the heart of Joshua. This same Word was also spoken to the New Testament church, *"I will never leave you nor forsake you." So, we may boldly say: "The LORD is my helper; I will not fear. What can man do to me?" (Hebrews 13:5b-6, NKJV).* The action of faith is a powerful access to the child of God. I am often quoting the meaning of faith that it is not a guess or something we assume. Faith is a Word from Almighty God, spoken into our hearts that we can live by and expect great results. When the Lord spoke to Joshua concerning his victory over the nations, he was going to fight against the nations as the Word of God had promised. Children of Almighty God we do not have to assure or guess if the Lord has given us the expected time that He will carry out His plan. This is faith assured in the heart of every spirit-filled believer. I believe every child of Almighty God should know the voice of the Lord and seek to hear what the Lord God is saying to us. The Lord is our leader and guide. He will speak to us often to assure us of the promises He has made. Our job as believers is to have sufficient faith (little faith) that we might see the glory of Almighty God proven in our lives. When we read the book of Joshua, we can expect great things because the evidence of faith is great in the heart of Joshua. If you are called by the Lord to be a Christian leader it is important that faith is a necessary aspect of your life as a Christian. Remember the scripture: ***"But without faith it is impossible to please Him..." (Hebrews 11:6a, NKJV).*** Consider this concept: the Lord God that made everything that exists continues to bless His most treasured creation, mankind. The Lord God is not only asking us to believe but to also act on the Word spoken to us. This concept is what makes children of God great. Hear God, believe God, and act on what the Lord God has said! These three concepts (hearing, believing, and acting) are three important factors that cannot be left out of our Christian walk in Christ. When we read **Hebrews 11,** our level of faith should increase, and we (Christians) should move from one degree of glory to another.

We will encounter great success in our spiritual battles and yet if in some battles we may fail, we should return to the battle, continue to fight, and win! The life of Joshua is evident of the struggle of one such failure which was caused by the man, named Achan in Joshua's army. When Joshua and his army moved from Jericho to conquer the next battle, which is the city of Ai, there was trouble in the camp. Joshua was not the reason for the trouble. But the trouble was introduced by a man named

Achan. It is interesting when we read the life of Achan, that he was of the tribe of Judah. Note the scriptures: *"But the children of Israel committed a trespass regarding the accursed things, for Achan the son of Carmi, the son of Zabdi, the son of Zerah, of the tribe of Judah, took of the accursed things; so the anger of the Lord burned against the children of Israel." (Joshua 7:1, NKJV).* After reading this scripture, I was amazed that Achan was of the tribe of Judah. Nevertheless, it is not your spiritual heritage that you are a part of but your individual commitment to the Lord God in doing the specific work that you are instructed to do. The entire nation of Israel suffered because of the sin of Achan. It is important that every Christian be a watchman on the wall to discern the things that are going on in our homes as well as in the church. Yes, I know the Lord is merciful and filled with love, but there are some things that should not be among the household of faith. Remember the young man that was having an affair with his father's wife. *"It is actually reported that there is sexual immorality among you, and such sexual immorality as is not even named among the Gentiles—that a man has his father's wife! (1 Corinthians 5:1, NKJV).* When you read this story, you will be amazed of the punishment that was rendered for the ungodly act that was done in the New Testament!

Just like Joshua and other leaders, we may encounter

ungodly actions by others that will affect our lives. These actions are experienced throughout the Bible. Nevertheless, the child of Almighty God must be aware of things that are going on to ensure that the glory of God remains present over the people of the Lord. It is also important that the work of the Kingdom of God remains steadfast and continues to ensure that the power of the Kingdom of God be manifested on the earth. Joshua had a spiritual task to be done but it was interrupted by the actions of Achan and his ungodly disobedience before the Lord. Once the incident was settled and the children of Israel went back to doing the things that was required by the Lord, blessings entered back into their lives. The glory of the Lord settled back on their lives, and they continued to defeat their enemies and see the glory of the Lord. The incident that happens to Joshua and Israel continues to happen throughout the history of the children of Israel. It is imperative that Christian leaders and children of Almighty God be spiritually aware of the people and conditions around them. The spiritual decisions we make must be made based on the written and spoken Word of the Lord. Joshua continues to be one of the great spiritual leaders in the Bible. He lived a great life before God and expressed near the end of his military career this quote worthy of expression: *"And if it seems evil to you to serve the Lord, choose for yourselves this day whom you will serve, whether the gods which your fathers served that were on the other side of the River, or the gods of the Amorites, in whose land you dwell. But as for me and my house, we will serve the Lord." (Joshua 24:14, NKJV).* Joshua was a type of Christ. His original name is Hoshea, "Salvation" *(Numbers 13:8)*; but Moses evidently changes it to Yehoshua, "Yahweh Is Salvation" *(Numbers 13:16).* He is also called Yeshua, a shortened form of Yehoshua. This is the Hebrew equivalent of the Greek name Iesous (Jesus).

Five

THE JUDGES OF ISRAEL

The passing of Joshua did not leave Israel uncovered from the total wickedness that was in the earth. However, the book of Judges characterizes a disobedient and idolatrous people. Time after time they were defeated because of their rebellion against Almighty God and each other. There were no leaders like Moses and Joshua but there were Judges that oversaw and managed the commonwealth of Israel. The people during this time set aside the Law of Almighty God and did what they thought was correct. Consider the scripture: ***"In those days there was no king in Israel; everyone did what was right in his own eyes" (Judges 21:25, NKJV).*** During the time of Judges their leaders were military people as Samson and Deborah (a woman) that had armies that fought against the enemy. Judah was one of the first that the Lord chose to go up and fight against the enemy and win. After the conquest by Judah and Simon, the remaining tribes fought and won some battles but did not win all the battles they were engaged in. The Lord God was disappointed with Israel because during their warfare with other countries some of the tribes did not drive out all the enemies. The enemies of the children of Israel that were not driven out, settled within the tribes of Israel, and caused corruption and many to fall away from Almighty God. The children of Israel did evil in the sight of the Lord God by serving idol gods. The scriptures declare: *"And the anger of the Lord was hot against Israel. So He delivered them into the hands of plunderers who despoiled them; and He sold them into the hands of their enemies all around, so that they could no longer stand before their enemies." (Judges 2:14, NKJV).*

When Joshua died the Lord raised up eleven men (Othniel, Ehud, Shamgar, Gideon, Tola, Jair, Jephthah, Ibzan, Elon, Abdon, and Samson, and one woman, Deborah) who was also a judge over Israel. The children of Israel did evil before the Lord and angered the Lord because of their behavior. One of several occasions the children of Israel cried unto the Lord during their captivity and the Lord delivered them. There was no military leader like Joshua, therefore the Lord chose judges to oversee the children of Israel and lead them to victory over their enemies. Nevertheless, it seems as if once they were delivered from one enemy, they fell into the hands of a another. The ungodly actions of Israel led them into the captivity of their enemies. One of the main reasons for the failure and captivity of Israel was their serving the idol gods of their enemies. I wonder what was so enticing about the nature of false gods. It was obvious that the false gods had no power or authority. How could a human being with mobility and power, made in the image of Almighty God, bow down and worship an idol god that was made by human hands? Should these images have power over God's people when they are objects of wood, stone, metal, or other inanimate material? Let us consider the scriptures found in *(Acts 17:22-31)*. The Apostle Paul considered that the people of these religions had altars erected to many gods and one erected to the "unknown god." Nevertheless, Paul makes this statement to the men of Athens: *"God, who made the world and everything in it, since He is Lord of heaven and earth, does not dwell in temples made with hands." (Acts 17:24, NKJV).* Nevertheless, the children of Israel during the leadership of the Judges did some of the most unspiritual things we read about in the Bible. When we consider the love and mercy of Almighty God, we are informed how the children of Israel were delivered from the evil they were engaged in when they cried unto the Lord.

Each of the judges that the Lord raised up were military leaders or rulers of Israel that engaged in warfare or military strategy. Over many years, the Lord raised up Judges to help the children of Israel overcome the military power and wickedness of the surrounding nations. If we give some thought, how could Israel have such a great religious history with Almighty God and stray away and do the things that caused the Lord to be angered? Human beings are often influenced by the things that surround them. Reading the Scriptures allows us to somewhat understand the nature of God's people. Let us examine. The descendants of Abraham were few compared to the nations that opposed them. Ungodly nations were determined to defeat Israel because of their spiritual association with Almighty God, which was always a blessing to them. When leaders like Abraham, Moses and Joshua led the children of Israel against other nations, the people of these nations were fearful because of the presence the Lord was with Israel. Nations were defeated and great fear came upon these nations because of the presence and mighty power of the Lord. However, when Israel responded negatively to the Lord God, they were taken captive by ungodly nations and suffered under their leadership. Nevertheless, the love that the Lord God has for His people is greater than what we can ever imagine! We may not have done the extent of the wicked things that Israel did as explained during this book of Judges; however, sin is sin, and it cannot be justified in the eyes of people and the Lord. Throughout the book of Judges, the Lord God raised up twelve leaders or Judges to help Israel overcome the wicked nations that were destined to overcome and destroy them.

This same wickedness exists today. Many people on the earth are motivated by the devil to overcome and destroy the children of Almighty God. These people are jealous because of the blessings the Lord God bestows on His people (Israel and Christians). Many unbelievers become angered when the message of salvation is spoken. Nevertheless, the Word of the Lord will not be bounded or restricted by the devil. The Lord God is still the ruler of heaven and earth. The Lord God will not allow the devil to destroy His creation or the people He has declared as His sons. Spiritual warfare against the people of Almighty God will continue until the Lord comes and He regenerates the heavens and earth back to where He determines it shall be. It seems like a long and grievous war as we wait for the return of the Lord and the New Heaven and New Earth comes into being. Nevertheless, the born-again believers have been equipped with the Spirit of God to give us the overcoming strength and power to deal with the power of the enemy and overcome all the wicked devices that are used to destroy us. The power of Almighty God intervened in one of the most wicked times during the history of the Lord's people. However, the Lord God raised up eleven men and one woman (Judges) to fight the good fight and keep the Kingdom of Almighty God from failure on the earth. Let us briefly explore the lives of these twelve judges including their successes and failures that kept the Kingdom of God functional on the earth.

The twelve judges of Israel after the death of Joshua were: Othniel, Ehud, Shamgar, Deborah, Gideon, Tola, Jair, Jephthah, Ibzan, Elon, Abdon, and Samson. When Othniel became judge over Israel, the Bible declares about the children of Israel: *"They forgot the Lord their God and served the Baals and Asherahs. Therefore the anger of the Lord was hot against Israel, and He sold them into the hand of Cushan-Rishathaim king of Mesopotamia; and the children of Israel served Cushan-Rishathaim eight years.* During this time of captivity, the children cried to the Lord, and the Lord raised up a deliverer named Othniel, Caleb's younger brother. The Spirit of the Lord was with Othniel as he judged Israel and they had rest for forty years. Ehud became judge over Israel and yet the children of Israel did evil in the sight of the Lord. Nevertheless, Ehud led the children of Israel to kill about ten thousand Moabites and Israel had rest for eighty years. The next judge was Shamgar who killed six hundred men of the Philistines with an ox goad.

Each time the children of Israel did evil in the sight of the Lord, they were enslaved by other nations. After Ehud died the children of Israel did evil in the sight of the Lord and the Lord God allowed then to be enslaved by Jabin king of Canaan, who enslaved and oppressed Israel for twenty years. Deborah was the judge over Israel at that time and she sent for Barak to employ ten thousand men of the sons of Naphtali and of the sons of

Zebulun to fight against the enemies of Israel. Deborah and Barak went together to fight against the children of Canaan and defeated them. The Lord allowed the hand of the children of Israel to grow stronger against Jabin and the Canaanites until their enemies were destroyed.

The children did evil again in the sight of the Lord, and they were delivered in the hands of the Midianites. The Midianites would come up against Israel along with other nations and destroy Israel's land, crops, and livestock. The children of Israel cried to the Lord because of the treatment of their enemies. The Lord sent a prophet to speak to the children of Israel concerning their evil ways. The prophet explained to the children of Israel that the Lord God had done great things for them, yet they did not obey the Lord. Their disobedience led to their captivity and mistreatment by the wicked nations. The children of Israel hid themselves from their enemies because of the cruel things their enemies did against them. The Angel of the Lord appeared to Gideon and informed him how to defeat the Midianites that were oppressing Israel. The Angel of the Lord placed several tests before Gideon to prove his readiness to carry out the will of Almighty God. Gideon had thirty-two thousand men that were going to fight against the Midianites, Amalekites, and others. Nevertheless, the Lord informed Gideon that they were too many and the number was reduced to ten thousand and eventually reduced to three hundred, which is an unconventional means of warfare. Gideon and the three hundred men did what the Lord God had instructed them and defeated the enemies of Israel.

It appears to be a common trait that after a judge was chosen to rule over Israel and died, the children of Israel reverted to doing evil things before the Lord. *Judges 9-12* gives detail information about other judges that the Lord God used to direct Israel to overcome their enemies and restore order to the land of Israel. Nevertheless, the children of Israel did evil in the sight of the Lord again and were held captive forty years by the Philistines. The last judge who delivered Israel was Samson. The Lord God declared: ***"For behold, you shall conceive and bear a son. And no razor shall come upon his head, for the child shall be a Nazirite to God from the womb; and he shall begin to deliver Israel out of the hand of the Philistines." (Judges 13:5, NKJV).*** The history of Samson's birth through death is found in *Judges 13-16.* After Israel disobeyed the Lord and did evil in His sight, they were delivered into the hands of the Philistines for forty years. When Samson was conceived the Lord explained to his father and mother that he would grow up and become a Judge for Israel. Samson had great strength so that he could kill many men by himself and even the most dangerous animals. Samson was true to his calling, yet he was fond of the ladies of the Philistines. These ladies, like the men of course, were a part of the enemies of the nation of Israel. They were given council to entice and trap Samson to find out his great strength. During the time of entrapment by the women of Philistia, Samson used his God-given strength to do great harm to many men that were the enemies of Israel. During Samson's encounter with Delilah, a harlot in Gaza, she convinced Samson to tell her the reason for his great strength. Samson told Delilah the source of his strength and the Philistines took him, put his eyes out, bound him with bronze fetters, and imprisoned him.

When Samson's hair began to grow back, he cried to the Lord God for revenge against his adversaries. While the Philistines were celebrating the capture of Samson and playing sports because of his capture, Samson cried out for revenge against his adversaries. The Lord God allowed Samson to regain his great strength and he pushed the pillars he was chained to, and the place in which the Philistines were celebrating fell. The Bible declares that those that were killed during this event were greater than the enemies that Samson had killed before. The Judges were all, respectively, types of Christs in that they were deliverers and redeemers for God's oppressed people. Whenever Israel sinned the Lord sent foreign nations to punish them for their rebellion. When they came to an end of themselves and cried out to the Lord, He raised up a deliverer. In each case, the judges won the victory against the enemies of Almighty God and the children of Israel. While each of the circumstances were different, they each had an unlikely prospect and unexpected victory in common.

Six

RUTH—OUR KINSMAN REDEEMER

The Book of Ruth involves the marriage of a man, Boaz of Israel, with a woman, Ruth that was a Moabite. After the death of Elimelech, Naomi's husband, Naomi was left with her two sons, Mahlon and Chilion. These two sons married women, Orpah and Ruth, of the land of Moab. After a period of time Orpah and Ruth husbands died. Orpah desired to return to the land of Moab. Ruth desired to stay with Naomi, her mother-in-law. Naomi tried to convince her daughter-in-law to go back to Moab, but Ruth was determined to remain with her mother-in-law Naomi. Consider these words spoken by Ruth to her mother-in-law: *"Entreat me not to leave you, Or to turn back from following after you; For wherever you go, I will go; And wherever you lodge, I will lodge; Your people shall be my people, And your God, my God. Where you die, I will die, And there will I be buried. The Lord do so to me, and more also, If anything but death parts you and me." (Ruth 1:16-17, NKJV).* A Christian can consider these word that Ruth spoke as a type of commitment to Christ. Ruth realizes that there was something special about staying with Naomi and trusting the God of Israel when she said, *"Your people shall be my people, And your God, my God."* Ruth likely had envisioned or had a divine revelation that to remain with the children of Israel and Jehovah God would be the best thing that could happen to her. Remember, Ruth refused to go back to Moab with Orpah. Ruth's desire was to remain with her mother-in-law Naomi, which also meant that she would be among the people of Almighty God. The scriptures do not declare exactly why Ruth was determined to stay with Naomi and not return to her homeland. Nevertheless, her determination to stay brought about a great change in her life that lasted throughout generations.

Ruth was a Moabite that was willing to marry again into Naomi's family. What did she see in the people of Israel and the Almighty God that they served? There must have been something that greatly motivated her to stay and accept the religion and customs of the people of Israel. We do not know if it was what she observed in the people of Israel or the voice of Almighty God talking directly to her or the children of Israel. Have you thought about your life and the things in your mind especially about salvation? I believe the Lord God moves on the hearts of people to motivate them with His gracious love to bring them to salvation or a spiritual change in their life. Ruth had a choice to make that would affect her life and the entire generation of Israel. Boaz and Ruth are listed in the genealogy of Jesus Christ in *(Matthew 1:1-17)*. The marriage of Boaz to Ruth brought about the son Obed, who gave birth to Jesse, and Jesse gave birth to David the king of Israel. Through the succession of David, we have our Lord Jesus Christ who is the only begotten son of God. The Lord God used men and women to bring about the Savior of the world to redeem men and women from the curse of the Law and bring them to a state of redemption through our Lord Jesus Christ.

Ruth was a Moabite, a part of the family of Israel through Lot, the nephew of Abraham. The Moabites belonged to the same ethnic stock as the Israelites. Their ancestral founder was Moab, a son of Lot. However, the Moabites fought against their own relatives, the sons of Israel. You may say that they were distant cousins, yet still under the family of Abraham. It is amazing how the Lord God can bring people together and unite them for a common good for all mankind. When we read the history of Israel, we find that they fought against the people of Moab. Yet after all this fighting the Lord God brings them together to be a part of the family of our Lord Jesus Christ. I believe the Lord God is uniting all people to come together to be ready when He returns to take His children out of the earth into the Kingdom of Heaven! Unfortunately, we live in a world that is so divided by race, creed, and cultures. We make it known to all people that we are different and especially unique in our differences. This may be true, yet we cannot declare that our culture is superior to others that are a different race, creed, or color. I have found that each of us are unique, and each of us bring something to the entire whole of the culture of mankind that makes us strong, intelligent, and wise. The uniqueness of cultures adds to the wisdom and structure of our society. When we study the history of mankind, we can easily determine that the coming together of all people gives us an intellectual view to the growth and development of good things in the earth. What if we used this natural and spiritual wisdom to walk in unison with each other and Almighty God? Such wisdom would change the world and even blot out the wickedness of the devil that remains as the primary source which separates us from each other and from Almighty God.

When we consider the great things that have been accomplished in the earth it is well known that people came together and shared their ideas to design great things in the earth. The Lord God made each of us unique and gave mankind the ability to create and design things that would benefit the entire human race. However, the wisdom we possess is being changed by the devil for evil and destruction. I believe we can turn around this natural and evil phenomenon to a godly direction that will be beneficial to all mankind. The concepts that I have talked about are not impossible but will not happen as long as humans are under the control of the evil one. The Lord God knew that evil conditions would dominate the earth because of Adam's disobedience and fall from grace. However, the Lord God gave us another chance to move out from the domain of the devil by allowing us to be born-again by the Spirit of the Lord. The new-birth process is the most important spiritual reformation designed for mankind. Note the scripture: *"Beloved, now we are children of God; and it has not yet been revealed what we shall be, but we know that when He is revealed, we shall be like Him, for we shall see Him as He is. And everyone who has this hope in Him purifies himself, just as He is pure." (1 John 3:2-3, NKJV).* What an amazing consolation of hope for the children of God through our Lord Jesus Christ! Each day we travel through this world we find hope and yet we experience times of despair because we still must deal with the nature of Adam within ourselves (saved yet still in the flesh) and by others (unsaved and apart from God). The Word of God declares: *"For we do not wrestle against flesh and blood, but against principalities, against powers, against the rulers of the darkness of this age, against spiritual hosts of wickedness in the heavenly places." (Ephesians 6:7, NKJV).* When we consider this scripture, we realize what we are fighting against and the magnitude of our fight and the power within us that fights on our behalf. We are fighting a spiritual fight, yet we have been equipped with the spiritual weapons from the Lord to fight effectively and win the fight.

When the Lord God decided to bring salvation through Himself, He realized that the forces of the adversary would be against us and Him. Every type of Christ was met with conflict and adversity to slow down or try to stop the movement of the will of God from coming to earth to save mankind. Nevertheless, Almighty God could not be stopped! The love that He had for mankind led Him to the cross of Calvary to die as the only acceptable sacrifice that would destroy the works of the devil. Just as we read the story of Ruth, she was determined not to go back to the land of Moab after her husband died. However, she was determined to remain with her mother-in-law. The scriptures do not indicate whether she heard the voice of the Lord or not. But she was determined to stay with her mother-in-law as long as time permitted. Her determination allowed her to be included in the genealogy of Jesus Christ, and the great grandmother of the patriarch David. What a great legacy that included Ruth the Moabite! Have you ever thought about your legacy in Christ Jesus? Have you been instructed by the Holy Spirit to speak to others about the saving grace of our Lord Jesus? I believe if you take heed to the Word of the Lord and witness to someone about the saving grace of our Lord Jesus Christ, it will set off a chain-reaction of salvation! They will receive the gift of salvation; the Lord will be proud of you for being a bonified witness that has brought someone into the Kingdom of God. Give serious thought to what I am saying. The Lord said: ***"But you shall receive power when the Holy Spirit has come upon you; and you shall be witnesses to Me in Jerusalem, and in all Judea and Samaria, and to the end of the earth." (Acts 1:8, NKJV).*** When we are filled with the Holy Spirit, we have the power to speak to other people and encourage them to give their lives to the Lord and receive the Holy Spirit. Our work in Christ just begins when we are saved by the Blood of Jesus Christ. I pray each day that the Lord would direct someone to me or direct me to someone that I may witness salvation and pray that they will give their lives to the Lord. Consider this scripture concerning Ruth and the birth of a son: ***"Then the women said to Naomi, "Blessed be the Lord, who has not left you this day without a close relative; and may his name be famous in Israel!" (Ruth 4:14, NKJV).*** I pray that all born-again believers will be willing to consider the Word of the Lord and do the work that the Lord has impressed on you to do; causing others to hear the Word of the Lord and be born again!

Seven

DAVID THE GREAT GRANDSON OF BOAZ AND RUTH

David, the King of Israel is the great grandson of Boaz and Ruth. David was a great man of war that delivered Israel out of the hands of the Philistines through many wars and especially out of the hands of the giant Goliath. David as the leader of Israel, fought many wars against the Philistines. David was in conflict with Saul, the first king of Israel. Saul desired to kill David because when they returned from war, the rejoicing of the women of Israel declared David's greater victory specifying ten-thousands, and Saul's victory of only a thousand. *(1 Samuel 18:6-7).* Saul was very displeased as the women referred to David's great victory compared to Saul's lesser victory. The jealousy of Saul towards David led Saul to try to kill David. When Saul died, David eventually became the king of Israel. David's leadership over Israel led them to become a great and powerful nation during that time. Many things were done to enhance the Kingdom of Israel to be the leader throughout other regions around Israel. David built up the kingdom of Israel, so it became the admiration power and well-respected military power by other nations. David and the Kingdom of Israel was well respected and feared by other nations also. David was a man of war that dealt with Israel's enemies severely and gained respect because of his cunning war efforts and the many victories he won over the many enemies of Israel. The scriptures say that David was a man after God's own heart: *"...He raised up for them David as king, to whom also He gave testimony and said, I have found David the son of Jesse, a man after My own heart, who will do all My will." (Acts 13:22, NKJV).*

David was a man of God that was well respected in the scriptures. He learned the ways of the Lord and became a great warrior for the kingdom of Israel. Many of the evil and unrighteous kingdoms surrounding Israel were defeated and destroyed under the leadership of David. He kept his focus on Almighty God as he led Israel into battle against their enemies. When David was faced with difficult decisions, he presented these decisions before the Lord God for correct instructions and directions. Let's consider one of these trying times for David. When David and his army were out to war against the enemies of Israel, their enemies came invaded and destroyed their camp. The enemy took their families and destroyed their houses. When David and his men returned, they were devastated because their families were taken captive and their homes were destroyed. After David's soldiers had wept for a period of time, they wanted to stone David. David asked for an ephod (a special piece of clothing worn by the priest) and prayed. Consider David's prayer: *"So David inquired of the Lord, saying, "Shall I pursue this troop? Shall I overtake them?" And He answered him, "Pursue, for you shall surely overtake them and without fail recover all." (1 Samuel 30:8, NKJV).* David's prayer was answered. Just as the Lord said, David recovered all the material things, livestock, and their wives. I am very concerned about the children of Almighty God during this time. Many have concluded that the Lord does not speak to them. I have answered this question before and will continue to declare it as many times as I can, the Lord speaks to His children! Just read the scriptures. Throughout the Bible we are informed that the Lord spoke to His children, and they were successful because of what the Lord was saying to them.

David was willing to do the things that the Lord wanted him to do. He was willing to fight many battles to overcome the enemies of Israel. Are we willing to pray and fast to defeat the enemy that our brothers and sisters in Christ might be released from the bondage of the devil? Remember we do not fight just for ourselves, but for the whole Body of Christ. Many of our brethren are struggling with spiritual wars constantly coming against them. It is important that we remember that we are a body of believers. When we consider that we are the Body of Christ we realized that we are connected to each other. If one member is hurting the whole body is affected. David could not effectively win all these battles by himself. He needed the help of others to win the battles and eventually win the war. We cannot stand alone or with a select group of individuals if we are going to win the spiritual battles that come against the whole Body of Christ. David did not win all these great battles by himself. He had great men of war that fought with him and helped him fight and win. I believe we are all in this spiritual fight together. We are together as a team of believers fighting the good fight of faith and looking forward to winning and receiving the spoils of our victory! However, I believe that we are driven by our faith in the word of Almighty God. We cannot obtain the ultimate victory unless we believe the Written Word, hear the Spoken Word, and act on both. The Lord wants us to be assured what He has spoken, and our faith drives us to the victory. We are children of Almighty God, and the Lord continues to speak to His children that we may be victorious in every walk of our lives. Why was David so successful? He heard the voice of the Lord and acted on what was written and spoken. I advise many of my readers to consider what I have just said. Our spiritual success is the Word of the Lord written and spoken. How do we achieve these profound spiritual acts? The Written Word has been given to us through the Bible. This document (the Bible) is not just for historical purposes. It is the Word of the Lord to guide our lives. The more we read this sacred document the more insight we get into the mind of Almighty God. We also learn how to pray and fight the enemy of our souls. The other means of gaining access to the voice of Almighty God is praying. Praying is not just a monologue (your voice only to the Lord), but a dialogue. We speak to the Lord, and He speaks back to us. When I read the scriptures, I think about the example of Joshua asking the Lord for an answer as to the military failure at Ai. *(Joshua 7:5)*. The Lord God gave Joshua the reason for the military failure. The Lord answered, and the problem was corrected! It is unfortunate that many children of God do not think that the Lord speaks to them. I wonder why? Perhaps they do not want the Lord to answer because of what may be said that will alter their lifestyle. I pray that what I am saying will help someone on their spiritual journey and lead them to great success that will help them throughout their spiritual and natural lives.

When we consider the actions of David, we understand that he was a man after God's own heart. *(Acts 13:22)*. Reading about David in the scriptures gives us an understanding how he expressed his loyalty to Almighty God and to the people he was serving.

What a great example we have in the scriptures to follow! When David's men were willing to kill him for the tragedy that occurred to their camp while they were away fighting, he immediately made his petition before the Lord. When the Lord answered, David did not hesitate to do what the Lord told him to do. This is why such heroes of faith are listed in the Bible for Almighty God's people to read, consider, and act upon. When I read such actions of the heroes of faith I am motivated to go beyond the natural actions of mankind and go into the spiritual actions that Almighty God places in my heart. Many of our churches have become political and have left out the spiritual movement that is required by Almighty God. When I hear the Word of the Lord I am motivated by the scriptures and not the natural things that are expressed by the doctrines of human beings. When we read about David and other heroes of faith, we understand their spiritual motivation and commitment to the Word of Almighty God. David and others mentioned as heroes of faith did great and impossible things because they were instructed by the Lord and believed that such mandates would be accomplished. Unfortunately, in the day in which we live we do not consider the voice of the Lord to be a part of our communication as children of God. I would like you to consider this scripture as a child of God: *"My sheep hear My voice, and I know them, and they follow Me." (John 10:27, NKJV).* Remember when the

Lord spoke to Saul (Paul after conversion, in the New Testament), when he was on his way to Damascus to punish the saints for serving Jesus? How can anyone misinterpret or disallow this and other scriptures concerning the Lord Jesus speaking to His people? When we read about the other heroes of faith *(Hebrews 11)* and other children of Almighty God, we read clearly about the Lord speaking directly to His children to accomplish great and specific tasks. Consider these examples: Almighty God spoke to Abraham concerning the offering of his son Isaac. *(Genesis 22:1-2).* Also, there is another example where Almighty God spoke to Moses at the burning bush. *(Exodus 3:3).* There are many others as Joshua, Gideon, and the Prophets, that were willing to be obedient and listen to Almighty God and do the specific things that the Lord wanted them to do. If we considered any of the heroes of faith it will prove the point of the Lord speaking to His children; and His children acting on Almighty God's spoken word to accomplish the desired task. I do not speak about the saints in the Bible only but about the children of God living during this day. I will use others and myself as examples to prove the point of Almighty God speaking to individuals a word of faith to show the wonderful works of the Lord. When we read about the heroes of faith in the scriptures and even the people of Almighty God during our time, we should be spiritually motivated to act on the word of faith that the Lord is giving us. I believe through the reading of the Bible and listening to the Lord speaking to us that we will gain the necessary faith (faith comes by hearing) to accomplish some of the great spiritual achievements that will please the Lord and benefit our lives.

Eight

TYPES OF CHRIST AND HEROES OF FAITH

When we read the entire eleventh chapter of the book of Hebrews, we clearly understand the movement of Almighty God working in the hearts of His children. When we read about these heroes of faith in the book of Hebrews and throughout the Old and New Testament, we can clearly see the Holy Spirit working in them to accomplish the desired task that the Lord wanted them to do. When we read about Seth, Enoch, Noah, Abraham, Isaiah, Ester, Deborah, and others in the book of Genesis through the book of Malachi, it is obvious that the Lord spoke to these men and women to move the spiritual accomplishments along through the time of the birth, death, resurrection, and ascension of our Lord Jesus Christ. There are many types of Christs that are mentioned in the Old Testament. Two of the main characters of the Old Testament are Enoch and Elijah. The reason I specify these two is because they were righteous men of God that did not die but were transfigured into heaven and did not see death. I will list a few Old Testament characters that are a type of Christ.

Adam was the first man that God created. He was the beginning of all humanity. God gave Adam the ability to name all the animals. The Lord God placed Adam in the Garden of Eden. Adam is explicitly said to have been a *type* of Christ in that he was the representative of humanity (***Romans 5:12).*** Paul unfolds one of the foremost ways in which he was a type of Christ in ***Romans 5:12-21.*** Adam's federal headship–together with the guilt, corruption, and death that his disobedience brought on all humanity–is contrasted with the federal headship of Christ, and the subsequent justification of believers through His obedience and substitutionary death. Adam is also seen as a type of Christ in *1 Corinthians 15* where his earthly body is contrasted with the resurrected body of the glorified Christ and His people. In both of these places there is similarity and contrast in the type.

Abel was the second of two sons born to Adam and Eve. Abel was the son that gave an acceptable offering to God. Both sons, Cain and Abel submitted an offering to God as was required. God accepted Abel's offering but rejected Cain's. Cain killed his brother Abel because the Lord accepted Abel's offering and rejected his offering.

Abel's correct worship of God through his offering led his brother Cain to become angry with God and directed his anger towards his brother. Charles Spurgeon said, *"If Cain could have gotten at the throat of God (figuratively) he would have done so. Nevertheless, Cain killed his brother Abel because of his anger towards Abel and God. Abel is compared with Christ because he was martyred as Christ was for righteousness."* There are two major things that declare Abel as a type of Christ; he was righteous, and he was killed because of his righteousness.

Seth was born replacing the death of his brother Abel. Consider the scripture: ***"And Adam knew his wife again, and she bore a son and named him Seth, "For God has appointed another seed for me instead of Abel, whom Cain killed." And as for Seth, to him also a son was born; and he named him Enosh. Then men began to call on the name of the LORD. (Genesis 4:25-26, NKJV).*** Even though Cain killed Abel the seed of the woman would continue through Seth. Notice: the purpose of Almighty God will continue regardless of what man, or the devil does to stop the purpose of the Lord God. Consider the end of ***Genesis 4:26, ...Then men began to call on the name of the LORD.*** The greatness and sovereignty of God may be challenged but never defeated!

Enoch was the great-great grandson of Seth. The scriptures declare: ***"Enoch walked faithfully with God; then he was no more, because God took him away. (Genesis 5:24, NIV).*** The Lord God did not allow the chain of righteousness to be broken. It was the determine will of Almighty God to ensure the righteous will of the Lord not be broken from one generation to another. The perfect will of God was to establish a righteous seed that would continue through time until the Seed of the woman would be produced (Jesus Christ)! Enoch being taken away to heaven compares to the resurrection and ascension of our Lord Jesus Christ. Enoch was not killed as our Lord Jesus, but he identified with the righteous living and accession of Christ Jesus!

Melchizedek was a type of Christ in that he was the King/Priest who blessed Abraham. No one in the Old Testament serves in both offices. Jesus is the Prophet, Priest, and King of His church. Melchizedek typified Him in two of the three offices *(Zechariah 6:12-13)*. Melchizedek was "King of Righteousness" and "King of Salem (Peace)." Jesus is the King in whom "righteousness and peace kiss" at the cross *(Psalms 85:10)*. Like Melchizedek before Him, Jesus had "no beginning of days, nor end of life." He is the eternal Priest to whom Melchizedek pointed. He was never, and never will be, replaced as High Priest of the Church.

Noah was a type of Christ because Almighty God gave him re-creative instructions as he was to carry the animals onto the Ark during the flood. When the rain ceased and the waters abided on the earth, the animals on the Ark were released. God gave Noah re-creation mandates to be fruitful and multiply. Consider what the Lord God said to Noah: *"So God blessed Noah and his sons and said to them: "Be fruitful and multiply and fill the earth." (Genesis 9:1, NKJV).* Noah was like Adam in that he was charged to oversee the mission of God's work and he gathered all the animals that the Lord God required; and to oversee the safety of the animals and his family that would replenish the earth. The earth that Noah inhabited after the flood was like a new creation. Noah was like a second Adam (Jesus is actually the second Adam) with instructions similar to what the first Adam received *(Adam; Genesis 1:26-28, and Noah; Genesis 9:1-3).*

Job was a type of Christ in that he suffered for righteousness as God gave Satan the permission the afflict his body. The affliction of Job's body also caused the affliction of his mind. Job's affliction of his mind was the humiliation he suffered at the offensive actions of his wife and friends. Job's suffering is a type of Christ in the suffering and glory of our Lord Jesus Christ. Job went through similar testing by Almighty God as Jesus was tested when he was tempted by the devil. Almighty

God's testing of Job led to a glorious ending as he was blessed with greater things after his suffering than what he had before. Almighty God meant good for Job even though he suffered. *(Job 42:12)*. Christ sufferings was meant for the good of all mankind. When Christ died and rose again every human being had the right to access the Throne of God, repent, be filled with the Spirit of God, and be saved. Job was a righteous sufferer in the presence of his people. Jesus is the righteous sufferer in the presence of the whole world who shows forth the righteousness of Almighty God.

Abraham is best known as the father of faith. His original name was Abram. In *Genesis 12:1-3* God speaks to Abraham:

>*Now the LORD had said to Abram:*
>*"Get out of your country,*
>*From your family*
>*And from your father's house,*
>*To a land that I will show you.*
>*2 I will make you a great nation;*
>*I will bless you*
>*And make your name great;*
>*And you shall be a blessing.*
>*3 I will bless those who bless you,*
>*And I will curse him who curses you.*
>*And in you all the families of the earth*
>*shall be blessed."*

In the book of Genesis, Abram obeys the commands of God to leave Ur of the Chaldeans and follow the direction of Almighty God to another land. Abram bears a son with his maid, Hagar and calls him Ishmael. When Abram was ninety-nine years old the LORD appeared to Abram and let him know that His Covenant would be with Him. The LORD changed Abram's name to Abraham, indicating he would be the father on many nations and Sari name was changed to Sarah. Abraham and Sarah laughed concerning the birth of their son in their old age. The LORD informed Abraham that He would establish his Covenant through Isaac.

When Isaac was born and entered into his teenage years the Lord informed Abraham to offer his son Isaac as an offering to Him. Abraham obeyed God's order to sacrifice Isaac. This was a great test of Abraham's faith, though in the end the Lord substitutes a ram instead of his son. Abraham was rewarded for believing God. When Abraham obeyed God and was ready to sacrifice Isaac, He believed that God would raise Isaac up from the dead because the word of the Lord that he had received from the Lord, ***"In Isaac your seed shall be called." (Romans 9:7 and Hebrews 11:18 (NKJV).***

Isaac was a type of Christ in that he was the promised "son of Abraham." The promises of God were given directly to Abraham with respect to His son (offspring). Everywhere in the New Testament we are taught that

Jesus is the true promised son of Abraham. However, in the original giving of the promise Isaac was the promised son in view. The birth and life of Isaac also typify the Redeemer. Just as Isaac's birth was the result of the supernatural power of God so too was it a true form of Jesus. Isaac typified the Redeemer in that he is the only other human sacrifice that God commanded, and–though God stopped Abraham from going through with the sacrifice of Isaac, he is said to have died and been risen, "figuratively" *(Hebrews 11:19)*. Jesus, the true and greater son of Abraham, was sacrificed, raised, and returned to His Father.

Jacob was the second son of Isaac and Rebekah. When Rebekah had conceived there were two children in her womb, she realized that the two children struggled in her womb. As the two children struggled within her body, she inquired of the Lord about her children struggling within her. The scriptures declare:

> *And the LORD said to her:*
> *"Two nations are in your womb,*
> *Two peoples shall be separated from your body;*
> *One people shall be stronger than the other,*
> *And the older shall serve the younger."*
> *(Genesis 25:23, NKJV).*

The key point in this this scripture is: ***"The older shall serve the younger."*** The declaration from the Lord indicated that Jacob would become the leader over Esau and receive the inheritance (blessing) that was in succession with Abraham and Isaac. Jacob became a great leader as he walked with God. One of great events with Jacob was the wrestling with God and successfully prevailing and gaining favor with God. After Jacob's successful challenge with the Angel, Jacob was granted a blessing and his name changed. ***The Angel indicated to Jacob. "Your name shall no longer be called Jacob, but Israel; for you have struggled with God and with men, and have prevailed." (Genesis 32:28, NKJV).***

Joseph, one of the sons of Jacob, he was a type of Christ in that he suffered unjustly by his brothers as he was mistreated and casted into a pit to die. Joseph was removed from the pit and sold as a slave by the Ishmaelites to Egypt. Potiphar, the captain of the guard of Egypt bought Joseph. After being in slavery Joseph was freed and then exalted to second in charge by Potiphar, the leader of Egypt, for saving the country from the famine that severely affected all that were in Egypt. Joseph was well respected and very successful in Egypt until Potiphar's wife tried to seduce him. Joseph escaped the evil trap from Potiphar's wife, but she seized his coat and lied to her husband that Joseph tried to take sexual advantage of her. Joseph was placed in prison for the lie that was told against him. After a period of time in the Egyptian prison, Joseph successfully interpreted the dreams of the butler and baker that were in the prison with him. The LORD was with Joseph, and he was successful in all that he did. God allowed Joseph to prosper in all that he did. Joseph was favored in the sight of Potiphar and served him. Joseph was made an overseer of Potiphar's house. Joseph found favor in Potiphar's sight and served him well. Joseph typified the sufferings of Christ. He was envied and hated by his brothers, suffered at their hands, and was delivered as a slave into Egypt to a place of power over the most powerful nation of the world (Egypt) at that time. In comparison, Jesus the greater Joseph, was envied and hated by His countrymen and brethren, who attempted to murder him; then exalted to the highest place of power and honor to save the world by feeding them with the rich granaries of Egypt.

Moses was chosen by God to lead the enslaved children of Israel out of Egypt. Moses was born to his enslaved parents, Amram his father and Jochebed his mother. When Moses was born the midwives were ordered by Pharoah to kill the child of the Hebrew women if it was a boy. However, the midwives did not obey Pharoah's command and allowed the Hebrew male children to live. Pharoah was still determined to kill all the male children born of the Hebrew women. Pharoah issued a second command that all sons born of the Hebrew women be casted into the river. When Moses was born Jochebed his mother decided to keep him from being killed by the Egyptians. She made an ark to float on the river and had her daughter, Miriam to watch the ark to see what would happen to it. The baby Moses was discovered by Pharoah's daughter, and she decided to take him as her own. Moses was raised by Pharoah's daughter. When Moses was grown up, he saw an Egyptian beating a Hebrew. When he thought no one was watching he killed the Egyptian. However, Moses was noticed killing the Egyptian. He feared for his life and ran away to the land of Goshen. The Lord appeared to Moses through the burning bush and instructed him to go back Egypt and tell Pharoah to let the people of God go. Moses completed the command of Almighty God and led the children of God out of slavery, though the Red Sea on dry ground.

Joshua was Moses' assistant. When Moses died, Joshua became the leader of the Israelites and brough them into the promised land. Joshua and the leaders of Israel had to fight and defeat many nations to enter the land that Almighty God had promised. The Lord God (Commander of the army of the LORD) spoke to Joshua in the book of *Joshua 5:14-15,* preparing him for war against the land of Jericho and upcoming cities. Joshua was a mighty leader and warrior that led the children of Israel from city to city defeating the enemies of the Lord. One of Joshua's greatest conquests during his fighting against the enemies, was the Amorites. *Then Joshua spoke to the LORD in the day when the LORD delivered up the Amorites before the children of Israel, and he said in the sight of Israel: "Sun, stand still over Gibeon; And Moon, in the Valley of Aijalon." So the sun stood still, And the moon stopped, Till the people had revenge Upon their enemies. (Joshua 10:12-13a, NKJV).* Joshua did great things throughout his life as he and his armies conquered the enemies of Israel. Before Joshua passed away, one of his greatest commands to the people of the Lord was this, *"Now therefore, fear the LORD, serve Him in sincerity and in truth, and put away the gods which your fathers served on the other side of the River and in Egypt. Serve the LORD! And if it seems evil to you to serve the LORD, choose for yourselves this day whom you will serve, whether the gods which your fathers served that were on the other side of the River, or the gods of the Amorites, in whose land you dwell. But as for me and my house, we will serve the LORD." (Joshua 24:14-15, NKJV).*

Solomon was a type of Christ in that he was the "son of David." He was the initial fulfillment of the Davidic Covenant. Ultimately, Jesus was "the son of David" who sits on his throne forever. Solomon was King of Peace. Jesus is the King of Peace. Solomon was wiser than all the men who had ever lived. Jesus is *"the wisdom of God."* Jesus explicitly drew a parallel between Solomon and Himself when he noted that the Queen of Sheba came from the ends of the earth to see the wisdom of Solomon. Gentiles now come from the ends of the earth to hear and see the wisdom of the greater Solomon (Jesus Christ). Solomon built the Temple in Jerusalem. Jesus builds the true and greater Temple through His death, burial, and resurrection. Solomon brought peace, "from the river to the ends of the earth." Jesus brought peace in the fullest and antitypical sense "from the river to the ends of the earth.

Elijah the Tishbite is considered one of the greatest prophets of all times. During the time when Ahab was king of Israel. Elijah approached Ahab and informed him that there would be no dew or rain, by the Word of the LORD. *"Elijah was a man with a nature like ours, and he prayed earnestly that it would not rain; and it did not rain on the land for three years and six months. And he prayed again, and the heaven gave rain, and the earth produced its fruit." (James 5:17-18, NKJV).*

The Word of the LORD came to Elijah and told him to hide by the Brook Cherith where he would drink water, and the Lord will command the ravens to feed him. The Lord then told Elijah to go to Zarephath and a widow, commanded by the LORD, would provide for him. The widow fed Elijah with her limited supply of oil and flour, and Elijah declared as the LORD spoke to him that the oil and flour would not be used up! Elijah also revives the son of the woman that had become sick and could not breathe. Elijah prayed to the LORD for her son and her son was revived. The woman declared Elijah was a man of God and the Word of the Lord was in his mouth.

One of Elijah's greatest defeats of the enemy was when Ahab, the children of Israel and the four hundred and fifty prophets of Baal were defeated at Mount Carmel. Elijah challenged the prophets of Baal to use no fire to light the sacrifice, but to call on their god to light the sacrifice. The prophets of Baal called on their god and cut themselves from morning to evening to light the sacrifice, but nothing happened. Elijah requested that the altar and sacrifice that he made be soaked with water. Elijah prayed, *"LORD God of Abraham, Isaac, and Israel, let it be known this day that You are God in Israel and I am Your servant, and that I have done all these things at Your word. Hear me, O LORD, hear me, that this people may know that You are the LORD God, and that You have turned their hearts back to You again."* When Elijah prayed over the water-soaked altar, the Lord God heard Elijah and consumed the altar with fire. Elijah brought the prophets of Baal down to the Brook Kishon and executed them.

There are many other miraculous things that the LORD allowed Elijah to do that demonstrated the awesome power of God working in him. Time would not permit me to talk about many of the great acts of Devine power that the Lord worked through Elijah. Nevertheless, one last thing that must be mentioned is that Elijah did not see death. The LORD took him up into heaven by a whirlwind.

Elisha

Elijah found Elisha plowing in the fields working with twelve yokes of oxen. When Elijah passed by him, he threw his mantle on him. Elisha left the oxen and ran after Elijah, asking him to let him say goodbye to his father and mother. Elisha followed Elijah and became his servant. On several occasions Elijah requested Elisha to stay in a particular city while the LORD sent him to another city. However with each request by Elijah, Elisha replied, *"As the LORD lives, and as your soul lives, I will not leave you!" (2 Kings 2:2, 2:4, 2:6, and 4:30).* When Elijah was getting ready to be taken up, He asked Elisha what he wanted him to do for him. *"And so it was, when they had crossed over, that Elijah said to Elisha, "Ask! What may I do for you, before I am taken away from you?"*

Elisha said, "Please let a double portion of your

spirit be upon me." (2 Kings 2:9, NKJV). The Lord took Elijah up in a whirlwind in a chariot of fire with horses of fire into heaven. Elisha watched the event take place, as Elijah was taken into heaven. Elisha picked up the mantel of Elijah and struck the water shouting, *"Where is the LORD God of Elijah?"* When Elisha had received the double portion of Elijah's spiritual strength, he began to do many miracles. The water in a certain place caused death or barrenness. Elisha cast salt into the water declared by the LORD God that the water be healed. Elisha was introduced to a widow woman that could not pay her debits. The lack of funds would cause her sons to be taken away from her as a way to pay her debts. Elisha, by the power of Almighty God, caused an abundance of oil to be created and sold to pay off her debts. Elisha, by the power of the LORD, brought back the Shunammite woman son from death. There were many miraculous events performed that Elisha by the power of the Living God was done. Just to name a few, Naaman, commander of the army of the king of Syria, was healed from leprosy, and the ax head made to float. Elisha died, and they buried him. *"So it was, as they were burying a man, that suddenly they spied a band of raiders; and they put the man in the tomb of Elisha; and when the man was let down and touched the bones of Elisha, he revived and stood on his feet. (2 Kings 13:21, NKJV).*

Jonah heard the voice of the Lord telling him to go to Nineveh and cry out against it because of their great sins. Jonah was on a ship going to Tarshish to escape the presence of the Lord. When Jonah got on the ship going to Tarshish he went into the lower part of the ship and went to sleep. Remember this same action was taken by Jesus when He got on a ship and went down to the lower part of the ship and went to sleep. Jesus' actions were like that of Jonah. A storm arose and caused others on the ship to fear for their lives. Nevertheless, the Lord Jesus rebuked the winds and waves bringing great calm. When Jonah was tossed overboard into the sea the storm ceased. Jonah did not want to obey what the Lord commanded because the people of this country were Gentiles and Jonah was a Jew. Nevertheless, Jonah obeyed the Lord and informed the men on the ship to throw him overboard. Jonah was entombed in the belly of a big fish for three days and three nights. Likewise, Jesus was entombed in the earth for three days and three nights. Consider the scriptures: *"For as Jonah was three days and three nights in the belly of the great fish, so will the Son of Man be three days and three nights in the heart of the earth. The men of Nineveh will rise up in the judgment with this generation and condemn it, because they repented at the preaching of Jonah; and indeed a greater than Jonah is here." (Matthew 12:40-41, NKJV).* Jonah was a type of Christ by his actions to obey the

Word of the Lord to save an entire nation. Remember when Jesus was in the Garden of Gethsemane and said to His Father to let this cup (crucifixion) pass from Him? If Jonah had not answered the call of Almighty God an entire nation (Nineveh) would have been destroyed. If Jesus had not answered the call of His Father, to give His life on the cross of Calvary the whole world would not have the opportunity to be saved. Each of these actions to not answer the call of Almighty God would have meant the destruction of many people. Jonah for the salvation of the city of Nineveh, and Jesus for the salvation of the whole world. Nevertheless, each were obedient to the Word of the Lord that saved many people. There are other heroes of faith that I have not mentioned. However, we should consider the Word that the Lord has spoken to us that we should go and speak the salvation of the Lord to as many as the Lord directs us to do so. This is the first spiritual job that the Lord gave us as Christians. *"Go and make disciples."*

Nehemiah was a type of Christ in that he rebuilt the walls of Jerusalem. When Nehemiah was in the process of rebuilding the walls of Jerusalem, the enemies of God came and functionally said to him, "Come down." He responded, *"I am doing a great work, so that I cannot come down" (Nehemiah 6:1-3).* When Jesus was hanging on the cross, building the walls of the true Jerusalem, His enemies said, *"If He is the King* *of Israel, let Him now come down from the cross, and we will believe Him" (Matt. 27:42, NKJV)).* The greater Nehemiah responded by saying, *"It is finished."* Through His death and resurrection, our Lord Jesus Christ built the walls of protection around His Church.

What has the Lord spoken to you that will bring salvation to people? I believe our ultimate job as Christians is to tell others about the saving grace of our Lord Jesus Christ! We are called to be witnesses expressing the saving power of the Lord Jesus to every individual. We have been given the boldness to speak the salvation of the Lord Jesus Christ to everyone. I admonish each of you not to be ashamed and unwilling to tell others about the wonderful salvation of our Lord Jesus Christ! Remember, someone told you about salvation introducing you to repentance, baptism, and the infilling of the Holy Spirit. I do not think that our Christian duty is complete unless when we are informing others about the saving grace of our Lord Jesus Christ. If the Lord tells us to speak to someone about salvation do not be ashamed and turn away. Someone is just waiting to hear the Gospel of Jesus Christ, turn away from sin and live a life committed to the Lord. When the Lord filled you with His Holy Spirit, He gave you the power to witness. Consider this scripture: *"But you shall receive power when the Holy Spirit has come upon you; and you shall be witnesses to Me in Jerusalem, and in all Judea and Samaria, and to the end of the earth." (Acts 2:8, NKJV).* This is the spiritual mandate for all persons that have received the Holy Spirit! It is not by our power that we achieve this spiritual mandate, but by the Spirit of Almighty God dwelling in us.

Nine

WHAT MADE THESE HEROES AND OTHERS GREAT

Now faith is the substance of things hoped for, the evidence of things not seen. For by it the elders obtained a good testimony. By faith we understand that the worlds were framed by the word of God, so that the things which are seen were not made of things which are visible. (Hebrews 11:1-2, NKJV).

Throughout the eleventh chapter of the book of Hebrews we understand what made the heroes of faith great. God gave them a Word and they responded by believing and carrying out the mandate that was given by Almighty God. The scripture makes this declaration as it refers to Abraham, *"Abraham believed God, and it was accounted to him for righteousness." (Romans 4:3; Galatians 3:6; and James 2:23).* Three times this passage of scripture is mentioned, twice by the

Apostle Paul and once by the Apostle James. What made Abraham the Father of Faith? When we speak of someone being the father of something it gives them the authority of being the one that establishes the beginning of faith and maintains its legacy. Consider the beginning of Abraham's walk with Almighty God. Abraham is considered the *"Father of Faith"* and his walk with the Lord is the prime example to follow. When we consider Abraham as the "Father of Faith" it means that he gives birth to all of us who embraces his strong faith in God. Abraham also had the ability to follow the Lord consistently throughout his life and trust what the Lord was telling him to do. I am completely convinced as the scriptures declares that ***"Faith comes by Hearing."*** That means Almighty God talks to His children. When we hear a Word from God, we should be obedient and act on the Word that we have received from the Lord. Children of Almighty God cannot go around guessing about the Word of Almighty God that speaks in our lives. Does the Spirit of God live in you? Do we guess about our natural occupations? Do we guess about when or where we are going on a long trip? I don't think so! It is imperative that our natural lives are filled with real information and data that will guide our live to success. Our spirituality must be considered the same way. The doctor that is considered a successful surgeon spends years studying under the authority of doctors that are seniors that can give instructions to make incoming doctors great and successful doctors. The Word of the Lord instructs us that, *"looking unto Jesus, the author and finisher of our faith, who for the joy that was set before Him endured the cross, despising the shame, and has sat down at the right hand of the throne of God." (Hebrews 12:2, NKJV).* Jesus designed and perfected the Word in us that will leads to our strong belief and our actions that leads to successful victories as we walk in Christ! The heroes of faith listed in the scriptures laid the foundation for the church that we may be successful in our spiritual walk and life in Christ Jesus.

In each case these heroes of faith did the things that Almighty God required in their lives. They were faithful to the Word of the Lord that they heard spoken to them. Abel heard the Lord and offered the required sacrifice that was better than Cain's offering. Abel was declared righteous because of his response to Almighty God. I believe when the Lord speaks to His children, we all have the opportunity to make the proper choice before the Lord. Notice how Cain spoke to Almighty God when he was questioned about his actions towards his brother Abel. Cain's attitude was sharp and disrespectful towards the Lord. It seemed to be totally disrespectable the way he answered the Lord. I believe the actions of the Bible characters sheds light on the way we should act towards the Lord God, our families, and the people we associate with and come in contact with. Our time when we are alive and after we are gone on to be with the Lord, continues to speak to future generations if we exemplify the character of Almighty God in our everyday living. We have the Holy Spirit living in us that expresses the character and love of Almighty God. When people see us and witness our actions, they will identify something greater than just the nature of the natural person. When people notice something different than the natural man, they will inquire about what is guiding our lives. This will give us the opportunity to express the love of Jesus Christ in our lives by the Holy Spirit dwelling in us.

The key factors in the lives of the men and women of God listed in the Bible and specifically those listed as heroes of faith is their obedience to the Word of the Lord. They were also willing to carry out the task no matter how difficult. When Almighty God spoke His Word, these individuals believed what they were told, and acted on the Word given to carry out the task that they were given by Almighty God. When we read the detailed history of these heroes of faith and others in the scriptures, we find that they had a love for the Lord, and they were willing to carry out the plans that were given to them by the Lord God, just as He specified. Remember Isaiah the prophet when he was called by the Lord God to do a specific task? ***Also, I heard the voice of the Lord, saying: "Whom shall I send, And who will go for Us?" Then I said, "Here am I! Send me."***

(Isaiah 6:8, NKJV). It does not appear that Isaiah was hesitant to answer the call of Almighty God after the Lord God had spoken to him. All the things that were given to him and some others by the Lord caused them to move without fear in doing what the Lord God Almighty commanded them to do. I am often reminded of the heroes of faith partition before the Lord when they were faced with uncertain conditions before them. When they were faced with these uncertain and fearful conditions, they made their request before Almighty God. When David received an answer from the Lord, he was determined to go out and fight the enemy and be victorious. When we read numerous accounts of David preparing for battle, he prayed and requested directions from Almighty God as to what he should do. Think about this for a moment. How victorious would we be if we acknowledge Almighty God in every important or fearful situation that will come into our lives?

Let's consider a few important examples. When we consider marrying someone that will become a close part of our lives, do we make our request before the Lord or decide on our own? What about careers and jobs? I believe that when the Lord God is in our plans we prosper! The heroes of faith love and belief serves as a foundation that stabilized their success in Almighty God. When we read about their actions of faith it helps us to be stabilized in the faith. This moves us to do greater things and encourage others to accept the Lord Jesus Christ and become great warriors in the Kingdom of Almighty God. Our salvation is great and wonderful! Nevertheless, the war is not over. If we pay close attention to our battles, we realize that some battles are intense yet as the song declares by the writer John Newton:

> *'Twas grace that taught My heart to fear*
> *And grace my Fears relieved*
> *How precious did That grace appear*
> *The hour I first believed*

It doesn't matter how intense the battles get; we are supported by the promise of our Lord Jesus Christ through the Apostle Peter: ***"Therefore submit to God. Resist the devil and he will flee from you." (James 4:7, NKJV).*** The key to our successful victories is that we submit to the Lord God first, and our fight against the devil will be a great victory! Our everyday life must be submitted to the Lord and obedient to every Word that proceeds from Almighty God. When our life is built up on the Word of the Lord, we become spiritually strong and mighty warriors in Christ Jesus. If you are willing to fight you must be willing to train for the fight. Successful training will lead to successful victories. Children of Almighty God must be willing to be on the *offence (the action of attacking someone or something).* We attack the devil with the Word of the Lord! When we know, the devil is planning to attack, the Lord God will inform us and give us the authority and power to defeat the devil. As the scripture has declared, when we fight in the Name of Jesus (resist) the devil and he will flee from us. The devil may return but if you fight with the power and intensity that you fought with before, you will win the fight every time! Always remember that we fight with the Word of the Lord as our weapons of warfare. I admonish each of us engaging in spiritual warfare to fight using the whole armor of God and we will obtain the spiritual success that will effectively defeat the enemy. *(Ephesians 6:14-19).*

When we consider the great things that were done by these heroes of faith we often marvel and give glory to Almighty God. However, I want you to consider not the greatness of the person but the greatness of Almighty God in the person! This same concept also applies to us as children of Almighty God. The Lord works things in us for His good pleasure. No individual can take the glory for the things that the Lord is doing. These men and women were considered heroes of faith because they listened to the Lord, obeyed, and successfully carried out the specific plans that the Lord God gave them. What specific plan has the Lord given you? When we read about the heroes of faith, we understand that the Lord gave them a Word that compelled them to carry out the plan that the Lord made very specific to them. The specificity of these plans was the Word of the Lord; through the written Word, the Voice of Almighty God directly to them, and through individuals He chooses to deliver and encourage others to perform the Word the Lord God has given. When we consider the faith of these individuals, we realize that their actions changed a multitude of people, places, and situations. Consider this scripture that concludes about some of the heroes of faith: *"These all died in faith, not having received the promises, but having seen them afar off were assured of them, embraced them and confessed that they were strangers and pilgrims on the earth. (Hebrews 11:13, NKJV).* This same word may apply to some of us as children of God. Almighty God may give us a word of faith that may not come to pass doing our lifetime, but many years after the Lord has taken us out of the earth. If the Lord God gave the Word to someone it will surely be announced by those who received it. Consider this scripture: *"The Lord gave the word; Great was the company of those who proclaimed it:" (Psalms 68:11, NKJV).* Our job as children of Almighty God is to receive the Word by whatever righteous source the Lord God gives and continue to spread the Word of the Lord as He directs. When we read the Old and New Testament it is evident that this was the method that was given by Almighty God and used by the sons of God to spread the Word of Almighty God. The hope we have in us, by the infilling of the Holy Spirit will give us the confidence to gladly do the work we have been given to do.

If we build up our most Holy Faith in Christ Jesus, we will not be afraid nor relentless to witness to others about the saving grace of our Lord Jesus Christ. When we open our hearts to the Lord, we will not be afraid to receive and act on the Word. This was the kind of spiritual actions that was carried out by the saints before and after Jesus Christ came to earth. The Lord God gave a promise and allowed His people to believe and accept what was said. Allow me to explain something that I have mentioned before. The Lord gives His people a Word. Many people of Almighty God do not believe that He speaks to them. If this is the case, we have loss the spiritual fight that has come against us. When we read about the heroes of faith it is evident that the Lord spoke and they believed, and followed the Lord's directions. We will never be spiritually successful unless we hear the Lord and do what He says for us to do. Do not allow anyone to convince you that the Lord does not speak to His people! Our victory depends on it! The Bible talks about some of the heroes of faith that died but did not receive the promise. However, they believed what they were told by Almighty God and saw the promises in the future. What was so amazing about these saints of Almighty God was that they believed and declared that they were strangers and individuals that were just passing through in the earth. Can you declare that this earth is not your home, and we are just passing through? Can you visualize the heavenly home that has been established by Almighty God for those that have been born again? If your hope of a Heavenly Kingdom made especially for you and you can imagine the hope of your place for eternal life, read ***Revelation Chapters 21 and 22.*** We will realize what Jesus said in ***John 14:3, (NKJV): "And if I go and prepare a place for you, I will come again and receive you to Myself; that where I am, there you may be also."*** I do not wonder or worry about the future of my salvation that has been purchased for me by the Blood of Jesus. The place has been prepared and now the saints of Almighty God are waiting for the Lord God to return to earth and receive His church into Heaven. I pray that we are anxiously waiting for the coming of the Lord. We may have died in faith having not received an earthly promise but by faith seen the heavenly promise of eternal life. Therefore, we confessed that we are not of this earth and look forward to seeing the coming of the Lord Jesus. When we embrace the coming of the Lord Jesus, we are seeking a great and wonderful home that cannot be compared with anything we can imagine! I believe there will be no desire to return to this earth after the Lord has received us into glory.

When we consider all the heroes of faith in ***(Hebrews chapter 11)*** it starts with the preposition, ***(by)*** and followed by the word ***(faith).*** The dictionary defines ***by*** as, in the direction of. All the heroes of faith were moved in the direction of the Holy Spirit to accomplish the will of Almighty God. I believe we will accomplish great things in the Lord if we are moved by the Holy Spirit and continue to be obedient to what we are being told to do. Faith is a powerful force in the life of the child of Almighty God. We cannot please the Lord unless we have faith. Our success in Christ is dependent on the Word we hear from the Lord and the action we take to allow the Lord to work in us His good pleasure. *Hebrews eleven* is given to the church as a guide to help us understand the Mind of Almighty God and walk in power and deliverance. When these two factors are clearly seen in our life others will believe and express the need for salvation in their lives. If we have been saved for any length of time, we should have come to the realization that without faith it is impossible to please Almighty God. All the things that were explained by the heroes of faith were accomplished by faith. Our successes spiritually and naturally will be accomplished by faith. Remember, *"Without faith it is impossible to please God."* Do you want to make the Lord God happy? Hear what He says, believe what He says, and act on what He says!

Hebrews 11 concludes with: *"And all these, having obtained a good testimony through faith, did not receive the promise, God having provided something better for us, that they should not be made perfect apart from us." (Hebrews 11:39-40, NKJV).* When we read *Hebrews 11:39-40*, it is apparent that the Lord makes the connection between the saints of the Old and New Testament. There is a working together that allows us to fight and defeat the enemy during the end time. The work that the Lord has given us is not separate from the saints in the Old Testament, neither is the work we perform separate from each other dwelling in the time of the New Testament. Our working together creates a powerful force against the evil forces of this world. Many of us have come to realize that there is a continuous fight against good and evil. We also realize that we have been empowered by the Holy Spirit living in us to obtain victory when we fight. We have been declared by the Word of the Lord that we are overcomers! I am convinced that when we fight, we will surely win! Therefore, it is imperative that we fight the good fight of faith and obtain the prize the Lord has instore for us. Saints of the Highest God cannot be afraid! We will be challenged often by the forces of evil coming against us, whether by direct confrontation with the devil or by people being used by the devil. When we consider that the enemy has raised its ugly head, it's time to fight with all the armor that the Lord has supplied to us. When we fight, consider the greatness of the Kingdom that we will receive as a Heavenly bounty that cannot be compared with anything in this life.

Ten

MOVING FORWARD WITH SPIRITUAL AUTHORITY

Therefore we also, since we are surrounded by so great a cloud of witnesses, let us lay aside every weight, and the sin which so easily ensnares us, and let us run with endurance the race that is set before us, looking unto Jesus, the author and finisher of our faith, who for the joy that was set before Him endured the cross, despising the shame, and has sat down at the right hand of the throne of God." (Hebrews 12:1-2, NKJV).

There are three major principles that will allow the saints of Almighty God to be successful in our walk in Christ. As the scripture declares:

(1) *"Lay aside every weight, and the sin that so easily ensnares us." (Hebrews 12:1b, NKJV)* Saints

and sinners are faced with evil things that will try to cause us to fail and walk away from Almighty God. Saints are not excused from this process. The devil wants to keep the saints held captive and bring them back to the sinful state that had once held us captive. Nevertheless, I am convinced that if we stay focus in Christ Jesus, we will not accept the desire of the devil and keep living spiritually. When sin comes upon us it is imperative that we pray earnestly, fight, and walk away victoriously. Every sin that is common or hard to resist, we must deal with it by calling on the Name of the Lord and fighting effectively with the Word of the Lord. Jesus spoke to His disciples when they asked why some demons could not be cast out, He replied, *"However, this kind does not go out except by prayer and fasting." (Matthew 17:21, NKJV)* The Lord God has given us the power to overcome every evil force and every sin that tries to overwhelm our spirituality. However, we will not overcome trials by asking them to go away. The only reasonable spiritual solution is to fight with the power of the Lord God and win. Since the power of the Lord's resurrection thousands of years ago; that same power has been given to us through the Holy Spirit living in us. Remember what the scripture has declared, *"We are more than conquerors!" (Romans 8:37b).* With the Lord living in us and fighting for us we cannot be defeated. However, we must remember to lay aside everything that would hinder our walk and fight in Christ Jesus. The transgressions that we bring on ourselves will surely hinder our spiritual progress and fight. The enemy will try relentlessly to bring things before us that will cause us to fall before Almighty God. We may fall but it is imperative that we get up quickly and repent before the Lord God Almighty. This procedure is following the Word of the Lord. *(1 John 1:8-10)*.

(2) *"...let us run with endurance the race that is set before us." (Hebrews 12:1b, NKJV)*. You may have heard the expression concerning those who run long races. *"It is not a sprint but a marathon."* Unfortunately, many children of Almighty God get in a hurry after walking away from or fighting the enemy. When this occurs many become discouraged, turn around, and even give up. It is truly a marathon that takes time and patience. Consider this example. Would you want a doctor to operate on you that has only one year of medical school? I certainly would not! The average surgeon takes about ten to fifteen years before they are considered a seasoned and professional surgeon. If this is the case in the natural what about the spiritual? Whatever the Lord God has called us to do His will, He will fulfill His will in us in His own time. It is important that we do not become overly anxious and fail the grace of Almighty God in our lives. Anyone running a marathon must be patient. If you run too fast, you will tire out and

lose the race. If you are patient, you will conserve your energy for the end of the race and win. Likewise, if we are patient in the Spirit and allow the Lord God to give us the strength and ability to run and continue the race we will win. If you are looking forward to winning you will consider what the scriptures are saying to us and never give up!

(3) *"Looking to Jesus the Author and Finisher our faith." (Hebrews 12:2a, NKJV)* When we read the scriptures, we realize that everything concerning salvation was designed, completed, and implemented by our Lord Jesus Christ. When we are motivated to obey the Lord, it is the voice of the Lord that we have heard and the courage to obey. We gave our lives to the Lord as we were convinced that Jesus gave His life at Calvary. Also, Jesus rose from the dead and filled us with the Holy Spirit that we may be saved. There was nothing, and no specific work, we could do to bring salvation to ourselves. The only thing we could do is believe and be confident in the finish work of our Lord Jesus Christ.

The great cloud of witnesses that we are surrounded by gives us the ambition and courage to keep fighting regardless of the obstacles that get in our way. We should remember the acts of faith by this great cloud of witnesses is a testimony to encourage us. These acts of faith should encourage us to fight the good fight of faith and win the fight just as the previous saints did and won victoriously! It is the authority and power of Almighty God that gave the witnesses in the Old and New Testament the authority to carry out the task to ensure that the Lord be glorified. I have confidence in the Word of the Lord that the Lord has given power and authority to all of us a great work to do in the Kingdom of God. What is your calling before the Lord God? I do not believe that we are called just to do nothing. We are called to enhance the Kingdom of God by bringing souls to Christ. Remember the three individuals that received the talents? One received five, one received two, and one received one, *(Matthew 25:14-30).* The first two individuals received rewards for the talents that they had received and presented them to the Lord. However, the one that received the one talent did nothing with it, and he was called a wicked servant. Have you thought about the talents and gifts that the Lord has given you? If you know that you have received a spiritual talent from the Lord, are you doing what the Lord had informed you to do to increase your talents? Each of us should be persuaded to do the spiritual work the Lord has given us to do. There should not be anything that would hinder or stop us from accepting and doing the work that the Lord has given us. There should be great joy in doing the work the Lord has given us. The work that the Lord God has given us should be the greatest joy of our lives. When you take the Lord's work seriously, we can see a change in our lives and in the lives of others that we witness to. Great blessings are manifested in our life, and we see to glory of the Lord surrounding us. I admonish every child of Almighty God to diligently seek the Lord for the spiritual work He has given you to do for the Kingdom of the Lord God.

One of the amazing things that occurs in our walk in Christ Jesus is the ability to move forward with spiritual authority. When we grow in grace, we find ourselves maturing in the things that the Lord has allowed to be in our lives. I am constantly reminded of the scripture: *"...but grow in the grace and knowledge of our Lord and Savior Jesus Christ (2 Peter 3:18, NKJV).* Our maturity in Christ Jesus allows us to walk in perfection and help others to walk in Christ and show a level of maturity that will attract others to the Kingdom of Almighty God. Faith in the Lord God will help us to mature in Christ. When we are born-again our whole life changes because of the Spirit of the Lord dwelling in us. When we hear from the Lord God and accept what He says, our faith grows and manifest. When this occurs the Lord places us in positions of spiritual authority. Nevertheless, let us not be naïve thinking that this great spiritual power comes as quickly as we read about it. The Lord God will make and mold us into the spiritual person He wants us to be. We do not make ourselves. The best thing the born-again believer can do is request of Almighty God what is it that He want us to do. When you make this request from Almighty God you will be very happy in doing what the Lord has said and not what you or someone else has desired of your life. During my younger years I was glad that the mature saints gave me guidance for my life and direction to walk by the Word of the Lord. However, my greater spiritual direction came from those living and walking in spiritual authority. These individuals did not call me into ministry but gave me godly directions that helped me to move successfully into the call that the Lord had on my life. I suggest that everyone that has heard the call of ministry by Almighty God, to be patient and careful not to rush into things but follow the Lord's direction and great success will follow. If you will consider what the Lord has said, pray, study the scriptures, and remove all doubt and fear about the call the Lord God has made on your life. You will experience spiritual success and see the glory of God in your life.

I believe the Lord God's call on our lives is one of the greatest spiritual acts that we can accept from the Hand of God. Do not allow the enemy or the enemy working through humans to remove you from the greatness that the Lord has placed in your life. The ministry that the Lord God has called us to is a great life, and its rewards are even greater because you are helping others to achieve spiritual greatness and bring peace to others that benefits the Kingdom of God. Now that our lives have changed and we are helping others, let's think about what's next. Let's consider the great changes that took place in the lives of the heroes of faith and what great changes await us as we are committed to the spiritual task ahead.

Eleven

THE GOOD FIGHT OF FAITH

But you, O man of God, flee these things and pursue righteousness, godliness, faith, love, patience, gentleness. Fight the good fight of faith, lay hold on eternal life, to which you were also called and have confessed the good confession in the presence of many witnesses. (1 Timothy 6:12, NKJV).

In the beginning of **chapter six, 1 Timothy**, the Apostle Paul is admonishing the children of Almighty God to be content, at peace with each other, and live a godly life. Paul mentions that many children of Almighty God that desire to be rich have fallen into spiritual errors that causes problems. Let me highlight a few things that negatively affect our spiritual life if we allow them to become a part of our lives. *"Now godliness with contentment is great gain. For we brought nothing into this world, and it is certain we can carry* *nothing out. And having food and clothing, with these we shall be content. But those who desire to be rich fall into temptation and a snare, and into many foolish and harmful lusts which drown men in destruction and perdition." (1 Timothy 6:6-11).* The Apostle Paul makes it very clear that there are certain conditions in life that could hurt our spiritual journey. When we are content to be godly there is great spiritual gain. I am a firm believer that if the work of Almighty God is first in our lives, we will have the prosperity that God desires for us. Have you read the life of King Solomon, King David's son? When Solomon was made king over Israel and Judah, he prayed to Almighty God for wisdom in order to lead the people of God. The Lord God gave him the wisdom to lead the people of God, and riches even though Solomon did not ask for them. New Testament scripture advises us: *"But seek first the kingdom of God and His righteousness, and all these things shall be added to you, (Matthew 6:33, NJKV).* Solomon was content to be godly and led the people of Almighty God in the way that the Lord commanded. The Lord knows our hearts and is willing do great things in our lives spiritually and naturally. We must understand that the Lord God loves us and is willing to do great things for us. However, He knows our hearts and what we may do to hurt ourselves. The Lord loves us very much and will not allow anything to destroy us. Sometimes we may become angry with the

Lord because we see other children of the Lord receiving blessings that we may desire to receive. Nevertheless, the Lord God will preserve our lives so we may not be spiritually destroyed by the things that we naturally desire.

When we are content to be godly there are many things that the Lord God will keep in store for us until the proper time. One of the things that I have experienced for many years is the maturity of the child of God before the receiving of many spiritual and natural gifts. We can desire spiritual and natural gifts but not be nature or spiritual enough to handle them. The Lord God knows our desire and ability to master the gifts that He wills to impart into our life. We must realize that the spiritual gifts are not for show and tell. These spiritual gifts are for the edification of the Body of Christ. The God given gifts are to help others and cause them to be motivated by the movement of Almighty God in their lives. Carefully notice these qualities that indicate maturity in Christ Jesus, *...love, joy, peace, longsuffering, kindness, goodness, faithfulness, gentleness, and self-control. (Galatians 5:22, NKJV).* These nine spiritual qualities are listed as the fruit of the Spirit. It is the spiritual aroma, and taste of the fruit of the Spirit that allows people to be attracted to the qualities of God through the Spirit. When these nine spiritual qualities are demonstrated in us, it will guide others to maturity that are examples of Christ

Jesus our Lord and motivate sinners to be saved. Notice that love is first before these spiritual attributes. This is a very clear indication that the righteousness of our Lord Jesus working in us will express the glory of the Lord Jesus in the world. When unrighteous people see the glory of God working in and through us, they may ask the question, *"What must I do to be saved?"*

When people witness the godliness in our lives some may marvel as to how we are able to accomplish such a great spiritual thing and live what appears to be a righteous life. We are living in a time that righteousness seems to be decreasing and wickedness increasing. As we approach the "**Coming of the Lord**", this decline of righteousness is becoming very apparent. These acts of unrighteousness are right before our eyes. Such acts are in our families, churches, and governments. There seems to be no escape from the sinful and wicked acts of human beings. Does this sound like a familiar story in the scriptures? Yes, it does, the days of Noah and the days of Lot. If we read the scriptures, we will become familiar with the times and seasons before the *"Coming of the Lord."* Consider this scripture: *"But know this, that in the last days perilous times will come..." (2 Timothy 3:1, NKJV)*. If we continue reading, *2 Timothy 3:2-9*, we will find that many of the things that are described are happening in the day we live. When we observe these acts of wickedness how shall we respond? I do not believe that we turn our heads and do nothing. Yes, those who live these acts of wickedness may fight against us; but should we be afraid and do nothing in order to live a happy and content life? I don't think so! Why are we surrounded by so great a cloud of witnesses? Their lives have spoken to us, giving us the courage to fight and win as they did. Are you fighting and seeing the victory in your fighting? Remember, when we win, we desire to keep winning. Our faith grows and we become stronger in Christ Jesus. The stronger we become the more battles we win and the greater confidence we have to continue fighting. Let's consider the Word of the Lord: *Therefore "Come out from among them And be separate, says the Lord. Do not touch what is unclean, And I will receive you." "I will be a Father to you, and you shall be My sons and daughters, Says the LORD Almighty." Therefore, having these promises, beloved, let us cleanse ourselves from all filthiness of the flesh and spirit, perfecting holiness in the fear of God. (2 Corinthians 6:17-7:1, NKJV).*

Based on the scriptures we have just read; I am sure we find it necessary to give ourselves holy unto the Lord by removing ourselves from the sinful activities that are in the world. The more we read the scriptures we find it necessary to separative ourselves from those who engage in sinful activities. These activities will lead to gross iniquity and unrighteousness that cause spiritual harm to others and us.

When we read about the heroes of faith, we find that they not only had the ability to engage in the spiritual fight of their lives, but they were willing to fight no matter the cost. Let's consider one of the spiritual fights when three of the heroes of faith had no natural weapons to fight against the enemy. The three Hebrews, Hananiah, Mishael, and Azariah (Shadrach, Meshach, and Abed-Nego), were commanded to bow down to the image that Nebuchadnezzar had set up for all to bow down and worship. The three Hebrews boys refused to bow down and worship the image. Therefore, the king insisted that the furnace be heated seven times hotter than normal. Hananiah, Mishael, and Azariah would be thrown into the furnace to be burned to death. Nevertheless Hananiah, Mishael, and Azariah answered the king in this manner: ***"O Nebuchadnezzar, we have no need to answer you in this matter. If that is the case, our God whom we serve is able to deliver us from the burning fiery furnace, and He will deliver us from your hand, O king. But if not, let it be known to you, O king, that we do not serve your gods, nor will we worship the gold image which you have set up." (Daniel 3:16-18, NKJV).*** Consider the action of Almighty God rescuing His children from the evil actions of Nebuchadnezzar king of Babylon. These three Hebrews had no weapons, and they were bound. They had no means of a natural escape from King Nebuchadnezzar. Nevertheless, they were going to be burned to death in the furnace that was heated seven times hotter than normal. These three men of Almighty God must have received a Word of faith from the Lord God to boldly defy the king's order and be subject to the penalty of death by being burned alive. One of the things that is very impressive to me is the way they spoke to King Nebuchadnezzar with boldness and no fear.

I believe that the list of the heroes of faith continues until this day and until the coming of the Lord. Some of the saints of Almighty God are sleeping in their grave waiting for the Lord Jesus to return and take them to glory. Faith in the born-again believer does not stop with the heroes of faith that we read about in the Bible. Our life in Christ has a rich heritage waiting for us to see the activation of the Word of God given to us through the written and spoken Word. The Bible declares that we should, "...*fight the good fight of faith, lay hold on eternal life..." (1 Timothy 6:12a).* Why is it called the *"good fight?"* It is because we will win! How can we lose when we are empowered by the Holy Spirit living in us? If we know that we are going to win, should we not consider it a *good fight?* I believe every fight we fight in Christ is a good fight because we are winners! Remember the scripture, *"Yet in all these things we are more than conquerors through Him who loved us. (Romans 8:37, NKJV).* When the child of God wins a spiritual fight, they do not just win or conqueror the enemy. Our win is big, when we fight, our conqueror is great. What happens when great a championship team engages in battles against other opponents? They play with great expectation of winning! Our level of expectation when we fight against the enemy should be that we obtain victory. Our victory is not even close because the Captain of our salvation is our Lord Jesus Christ! He is the Ultimate Champion; therefore, we are ultimate winners in Christ Jesus. Each time we fight and win we enter a new realm of spiritual maturity. If you consider a champion in Christ Jesus, you are not afraid to fight because you are confident that you will win. Many of us have engaged in spiritual battles, losing some and wining others. Even when we may lose a fight the Lord Jesus Christ raises us, strengthens us, and lifts up our heads to fight again. Every fight we fight will be different but if we fight in the Spirit we will surely win and glorify the Lord God of heaven. My brothers and sisters in Christ Jesus, keep fighting the good fight of faith. The Lord God is with us, and we are assured of the victory! Please be sure that our pursuit is the righteousness of Christ Jesus, and we will see the glory of God in our lives. Let us be thankful that the Lord our God has given us the victory through our Lord Jesus Christ!

Twelve

ANTICIPATING THE COMING OF THE LORD

Now this I say, brethren, that flesh and blood cannot inherit the kingdom of God; nor does corruption inherit incorruption. (1 Corinthians 15:50, NKJV).

All born-again believers please adhere to the Biblical fact that what we are naturally made up of (flesh) cannot inherit the kingdom of Almighty God. There is a constant changing of our natural being to be ready to enter the kingdom of God. The flesh and blood that we see and cherish each day cannot and will not enter the Kingdom of God. The flesh and blood that we see and what stands before God is the nature of Adam and is the corrupt nature that Almighty God will not allow to enter the Kingdom of Almighty God. If we open our spiritual minds to our daily existence before God, we will clearly see the corrupt nature that is in us. Think about this for a few moments. There are things that come into our minds that we know are unrighteous thoughts. When these thoughts occur, it is necessary that we make the necessary corrections. Consider the scripture: *"Therefore, putting away lying, "Let each one of you speak truth with his neighbor," for we are members of one another. "Be angry, and do not sin": do not let the sun go down on your wrath, nor give place to the devil." (Ephesians 4:25-27, NKJV)* Yes, we have been filled with the Holy Spirit and striving to enter the kingdom of God. However, we must easily agree with the scriptures, that the nature that exist in us is corrupt and cannot enter the Kingdom of God. We must make corrections daily while asking for forgiveness; through the Spirit for sins we make not only against Almighty God, but our brothers and sisters. The Holy Spirit in us will make us aware of the sins we commit against the Lord and our neighbor. In addition to the sins against the Lord and our neighbor, there are sins we commit in our own minds that are an offense to Almighty God. No human being may hear us, but the Lord God certainly does and we must atone for the sins we have committed. Consider the scripture: *"If we say that we have no sin, we deceive ourselves, and the truth is not in us." (1 John 1:8, NKJV).* We lie to Almighty God, ourselves, and others if we say we have not sinned. Some years ago, during my walk in Christ, I felt I was doing spiritually great. Nevertheless, at the end of the day while praying,

I ask the Lord if I had made any mistakes that I needed to repent for. I thought that there may be a few mistakes that I needed to repent for. However, after asking that question before Almighty God, I was shocked and ask the Lord to show me no more! I was not aware that I had made so many natural and spiritual mistakes that offended the Lord and my brothers and sisters. Therefore *1 John chapters 1 and 2* are important to read, allow the Lord to give you an understanding and practice what the Word of the Lord is saying.

The goal for all born-again Christians is to enter the Kingdom of God when the Lord comes back to the earth and calls His Bride to be received into glory. This is what every child of Almighty God should be looking forward to. I believe our hope to be caught up to meet Him (Christ) in the air is motivated by the actions of the Lord working in us. The movement of the Spirit working through us, and others gives us hope and motivation to anticipate the Coming of the Lord by being ready. Our readiness motivates us to stay in the will of Almighty God by keeping ourselves pure and ready for the Lord's return. Unfortunately, many have gone astray and lost the readiness to receive the Lord Jesus at His coming. The Coming of the Lord Jesus has to be the greatest spiritual event ever! From the time of Adam until King David and all the others that were used by the Hand of Almighty God, the Lord has used His righteousness to pave the way of salvation to come into existence for all mankind. Throughout the history of mankind many that were born by natural birth were brought to the earth to speak to the sinful conditions of mankind. Some of these great men and women did their best and help deliver mankind from their sinful lifestyle. The human race did good for a while, yet they went back to their sinful conditions. Consider the Word of the Lord: *Previously saying, "Sacrifice and offering, burnt offerings, and offerings for sin You did not desire, nor had pleasure in them" (which are offered according to the law), then He said, "Behold, I have come to do Your will, O God." He takes away the first that He may establish the second. By that will we have been sanctified through the offering of the body of Jesus Christ once for all. (Hebrews 10:8-10, NKJV).* Many years from the time of Adam and Eve through the Mosaic Law, man tried to please the Lord through many kinds of offerings. However, the actions of humans did not please the Lord. Even the righteous actions of those that walked close to God was not enough to satisfy the heart of Almighty God. The Lord God had no pleasure in the offering that were presented to Him for sin. It did not matter what man did to cover or eradicate his sin. These sacrifice and offerings were only a temporary covering for sin.

However, the Lord God takes away the first order (the Law) to establish the second (Grace). Let us consider the word *grace - (in Christian belief) the free and unmerited favor of God, as manifested in the salvation of sinners and the bestowal of blessings.* Under the Mosaic Law man worked tirelessly to establish a good relationship with the Lord through different kinds of sacrifices and offerings. However, through grace a relationship with Almighty God was established through the love and favor of our Lord Jesus Christ. Was man's actions, under the Law, through sacrifices and offerings totally pleasing to Almighty God? No! Under the Law were the actions of man trying to please the Lord God through works. Man's actions did not always please the Lord. When we read throughout the Old Testaments it is clearly seen that the indifferent actions of mankind led Almighty God coming to earth Himself, in the form of a man, Jesus Christ, to be the ultimate sacrifice that would please the Father and deliver mankind from sin. The Lord's action of grace was freely delivered to mankind for the eradication of sin and unrighteousness. There were no burnt offerings of bulls and other animal sacrifices that would eradicate sin forever. Consider these scriptures: ***"For what the law could not do in that it was weak through the flesh, God did by sending His own Son in the likeness of sinful flesh, on account of sin: He condemned sin in the flesh, that the righteous requirement of the law might be fulfilled in us who do not walk according to the flesh but according to the Spirit. (Romans 8:3-4, NKJV).*** It was the spiritual mandate of the Lord to bring us to salvation by His grace and mercy. The Law could not do what grace and mercy could do to bring us into a righteous relationship with the Father. The Law taught us that we were spiritually inadequate to master the commandments that were given to us by the Lord. However, as we tried to follow the Law and failed, we learned a valuable lesson. We needed to graduate from the Law and enter into a true relationship with Christ Jesus that we may be justified by faith. As one scripture declare; *"**Wherefore the law was our schoolmaster to bring us unto Christ, that we might be justified by faith." (Galatians 3:24, NKJV).*** Thank Almighty God for sending His own Son to earth to die for us and give us a chance for eternal life. Now we can walk in the Spirit that has been given to us that we may please the Lord God and continue preparing to enter the Kingdom of Almighty God. When I read about the great sacrifice that was made for us through Jesus Christ my soul is made happy, and I will yet praise Him for His love He has for me! This song, *No Greater Love, by Smokie Norfolk* constantly reminds me of the Lord's great sacrifice:

> *There is no greater love*
> *No love nowhere, no greater love*
> *Than a man would lay down His life for*
> *a friend*
> *No love nowhere, I've searched all over*

This great love that the Lord has for us caused Him to give His life that we may live spiritually on earth and prepare to enter the Kingdom of God. We should remind ourselves; *"Now this I say, brethren, that flesh and blood cannot inherit the kingdom of God; nor does corruption inherit incorruption. (1 Corinthians 15:50, NKJV).* The physical state that we are in cannot enter the Kingdom of God. Also, the corrupt state we inherited from Adam will not inherit incorruption. Since we are flesh and blood, we must be changed to enter the Kingdom of God; and since our flesh is corrupt, we must receive incorruption to enter the Kingdom of God. However, thanks be to Almighty God we have been given the power to overcome the nature of Adam in us, by the infilling of the Holy Spirit through the new birth process. Thanks be to God through His Spirit we shall overcome our flesh and blood and the corruption that exist in our spirit. When our flesh and blood; and our corruption cease to exist, we will enter the grave or we are called into glory. We shall hear the sound of the trumpet of God and be changed. Consider the scriptures: *"For this corruptible must put on incorruption, and this mortal must put on immortality. So when this corruptible has put on incorruption, and this mortal has put on immortality, then shall be brought to pass the saying that is written: "Death is swallowed up in victory." (1 Corinthians 15:53-54, NKJV).* When we give detailed thought about the *Coming of the Lord* it brings excitement and joy as we look forward to the arrival of the Lord Jesus coming to take His children out of the earth. One of the most interesting things is we shall be changed in a moment, and in the twinkling of an eye. The mortal substance (flesh and blood) that we are made of will cease to exist, and the mortality that defines who we are will no longer exist. Remember how we became new creatures in Christ when we were filled with His Spirit? The scriptures verify the change that takes place in our life. Consider the scripture: ***Therefore, if anyone is in Christ, he is a new creation; old things have passed away; behold, all things have become new. (2 Corinthians 5:17, NKJV).*** Consider this as change number one. The fuel (Holy Spirit) that is added to the spacecraft (glorified bodies) causes it to take off is powerful and special for the children of God to reach the desired destination (Heaven)! The Holy Spirit is the fuel that is necessary for takeoff and continuous traveling. Nevertheless, before a car, rocket, or any moving craft begins its travel there is preparation and anticipation. The Lord Jesus has fueled us with His Holy Spirit so that we may travel efficiently to the destination He has designed for us. I pray that everyone that has been called by Almighty God is making preparation to meet the Lord at His return to earth. The glory of the Lord will be evident as... ***"we shall see Him as He is!"*** We will also leave this world behind and forever be with the Lord!

Thirteen

GETTING READY TO MEET THE LORD IN THE AIR

When we anticipate going somewhere that is far away from home or just a short trip, we make the necessary preparations to ensure a safe and enjoyable trip. Our plans and preparations are checked several times before we take our trip. Many of us have concluded that to have a safe and efficient life we must plan and work effectively to ensure success. When we think about it, just about everything that is successful calls for planning and effective work to ensure our success. Unfortunately, many people will not be successful because they leave out the planning process for most situations in their lives. Benjamin Franklin once said, *"If you **fail to plan**, you are **planning to fail**."* Whatever we do in life where success is expected, there must be proper and intense training. Successful countries have many strengths, but their ability to work with others, follow and learn from those who have organized and built effective working conditions is key. Are you working with other members of the body of Christ to edify each other and help them prepare for the coming of the Lord? This should be the goal of everybody believing person as we prepare for the Coming of the Lord.

Have you as followers of Jesus Christ given any thought to these conditions that may apply to born-again Christians? If we love Almighty God and love one another as the commandants declare, we will obey and see the blessings of our labor on earth that directs us into the Kingdom of Heaven. I am convinced that much of the natural success in our lives will also have spiritual meaning for us to follow. Therefore, the Lord Jesus used parables to explain the spiritual meaning to the people that were following Him. I am convinced that there are many things that are on this earth that reminds us of the coming of the Lord and to inspire the children of God to make the necessary preparation for Jesus' return. Consider some earthly examples that may help us to prepare for the Coming of the Lord. I was an athlete many years ago in college. The success of an athletic team depends on the study of the opponents, which includes their strength and weaknesses. During the time of understanding the opponent's strengths and weaknesses there is also a time to strengthen the physical body to be ready for attacks against our bodies. If an athlete is going to win there must be the mental and physical preparation that will give them the strength to win the game. Another factor that is also important in athletics is teamwork, support, and encouragement to each other, so as the fight continues as a team we win!

The story of athletics and winning is like our walk in Christ. Each day we are faced with an opponent and adversity called the enemy or the devil. The Bible informed us: *"The thief does not come except to steal, and to kill, and to destroy. I have come that they may have life, and that they may have it more abundantly. (John 10:10, NKJV).* The Lord God shows us the great difference between the enemy of our souls and the greater love Jesus has for those that except and love Him. Even though our spiritual fight is continuous; our victory and rewards are continuous also. If I go back to the patriarchs as discussed in *Hebrews 11*, we do not find any that turned away from the promise that was given by Almighty God. These men and women of Almighty God had conflict in their walk with God, but never gave up even though conflict was directly opposed upon them. We are children of Almighty God, and we are going to experience conflict and opposition as we walk in Christ Jesus. Why did the Lord God speak to us through the Apostle Paul and inform us: *"Yet in all these things we are more than conquerors through Him who loved us." (Romans 8:37, NKJV)*? What are these things? Such things as tribulation, distress, persecution, famine, or nakedness, or peril, or sword will not overcome us and make us turnaround from following the Lord Jesus! The Lord God has given us the overcoming power to fight and win. Remember, we exceed the power of just winning. We win big! When we notice a football score of 55 to 0, we will say that the team that scored 55 points won big and slaughtered the opposing team. Brothers and sisters, the Lord Jesus won big when He died on the cross at Calvary and rose from the dead. Jesus' death, burial, and resurrection were the greatest victory over the devil that ever was. His resurrection was triumphant (a great victory of achievement). Jesus' victory at Calvary was for the salvation of every man.

Please note what Jesus said to Nicodemus a ruler of the Jews when he was inquiring about salvation: ***"Jesus answered and said to him, "Most assuredly, I say to you, unless one is born again, he cannot see the kingdom of God." (John 3:3, NKJV).*** When we read or talk about Heaven, we are anxious about going to Heaven. Most people think or assume that there is little or no requirements to enter heaven. However, the Bible has given us the requirements to enter the Kingdom of God; **YOU MUST BE BORN AGAIN!** It has been declared that the Lord Jesus is the Author and Finisher of our faith (Hebrews 12:2), therefore how can we deny what our Lord Jesus has said? We must believe and act on the word of salvation that has been given to all humanity for salvation. Can we make changes to satisfy our feelings or what someone has declared? I don't think so! When the Lord makes a declaration who has the authority to alter or change it? Absolutely no one! We must stick to the heavenly script that has been given to everyone on the face of the earth who desires to enter the Kingdom of God; *"You must be born again."* Throughout time people have made small and drastic changes in the salvation process. However, I believe in staying with the original word that was given by the one that died, shed His blood, and rose from the dead, Jesus Christ, the Son of the Living God! I am convinced that the written Word in the Bible is true. I believe if every person believes and act on that word we will be saved. We will also be confident that if we abide by the scriptures, we will see the glory of God on earth as well as in heaven. The Lord will always be true to His people. He will not alter what He has declared as truth. We can believe and have faith in what the Lord has declared over our life. If we will believe and not try to change what the Lord has said, we will see and receive the greatest blessings of our lives.

The truth that was revealed to Nicodemus was the absolute truth that should not be altered or deleted! What happens when the absolute truth is altered or deleted in our natural lives? Consider if the water pressure or the electric voltage is changed from the recommended standard amount for our homes. Perhaps the appliances that use the correct water pressure and the precise electric voltage would not operate correctly. Have you ever put the wrong gasoline in your car? What happened? The car that required normal gasoline did not run correctly if you use diesel gasoline. The owner's manual declared, not suggested, that you use regular gasoline. Human beings make these mistakes often and suffer minor and sometimes severe consequences for their actions. When these mistakes are made, we are devastated and often heartbroken for the loss of time and money. Our reactions would be overwhelming if we listen to the doctrines of man and not the Word of the Lord concerning salvation. The other part of Jesus' conversation with Nicodemus is this: ***"Jesus answered, "Most assuredly, I say to you, unless one is born of water and the Spirit, he cannot enter the kingdom of God." (John 3:5, MKJV).*** The truth concerning salvation was not hidden from the world. We have been given the Word of the Lord to obtain salvation and be with the Lord in heaven and on earth throughout all eternity. The Lord wills that all be saved for He died for all. The divine truth of Almighty God is open and shared with all mankind. The Lord wants us to move away from the imprisonment of the devil and live spiritually free on earth and throughout eternity. Consider these scriptures: ***"For this is good and acceptable in the sight of God our Savior, who desires all men to be saved and to come to the knowledge of the truth. (1 Timothy 2:3-4, NKJV).*** Did you notice the part of the scriptures that declares, *the Lord desires all to be saved?* Look at the grace and mercy of our Lord and Savior Jesus Christ! Almighty God did not specify a certain group of people for salvation, but He wants all to be saved. I pray that if you are not saved, submit your life to Almighty God and call on the name of the Lord Jesus Christ for salvation. Give your life completely to the Lord and walk with Him as the Word of the Lord has declared. The Word of the Lord has not change and the process is simple. When you submit your heart to the Lord, He will direct your steps and lead you to the place where you can give your life to Jesus by repentance, water baptism in the name of Jesus, and the infilling of the Holy Spirit speaking in tongues as the Spirit of the Lord gives you the ability to speak! Just have your mind made up to leave this sinful world and live forever with our Lord Jesus. I pray you will remain steadfast in Christ Jesus and look for the Coming of the Lord. Each day my expectation grows. I am excited about my spiritual future! I will do as the Word of the Lord has declared. If we do as the Word of the Lord has declared, we will have great expectations of going back with the Lord Jesus when He comes. I suggest that we have our hearts fixed and our minds made up expecting the return of the Lord. How about you? Please do not grow weary and give up. Since the resurrection of our Lord Jesus and the infilling of the Holy Spirit, many have perhaps given up and turned back into the world.

I am convinced that I have come too far to turn around now! I know too much to throw it all away for something that will not get me into the Kingdom of God. Please consider, the most important thing is the love of God that cleanses us from all unrighteousness and sin, cannot be just thrown away and forgotten. I appreciate what the Lord has done. I know I was a sinner and the life that I lived would deliver me into the kingdom of darkness. The things that I have learned through the Spirit of Christ living in me will deliver me into the Kingdom of our Lord Jesus Christ. That assurance is the new birth process that has placed us with the infilling of the Holy Spirit. The new birth process in me assures me to live a righteous life and be prepared to enter the Kingdom of God when the Lord Jesus returns to earth. Are you ready? Have you given your life to Christ and living a life pleasing to the Lord? I pray that you are expecting the return of the Lord!

Fourteen

WILL YOU BE READY WHEN JESUS COMES?

And while they looked steadfastly toward heaven as He went up, behold, two men stood by them in white apparel, who also said, "Men of Galilee, why do you stand gazing up into heaven? This same Jesus, who was taken up from you into heaven, will so come in like manner as you saw Him go into heaven." (Acts 1:10-11, NKJV).

Since the ascension of our Lord Jesus Christ, born-again believers have been expecting the return of our Lord Jesus Christ. Many great signs and wonders have occurred in the earth that have motivated the believers to continue to believe and expect the Coming of the Lord. Signs and wonders have happened since the resurrection of our Lord Jesus Christ. I believe that such signs and wonders will continue until the Lord returns and receives His church out of the earth and into Heaven. There are many people that do not believe that our Lord Jesus Christ gave His life to save us from sin and give us the right to enter into the Kingdom of God. Unfortunately there are many Christians of this day that do not believe that signs and wonders exist as it did in the days of the Apostles. Consider this scripture: ***"Now He did not do many mighty works there because of their unbelief. (Mark 13:58, NKJV).*** Some of the Bible historians of the past and during this day do not believe in the miracles that are performed by our Lord Jesus Christ. One of the basic acts of faith is believing. Remember the Words of the Lord Jesus, ***Jesus said to him, "If you can believe, all things are possible to him who believes." (Mark 9:23, NKJV).*** The time in which we live has grown cold towards believing in the coming of the Lord and living a righteous life. Unfortunately, many born-again believers have stop believing in the miraculous power of the Lord and has settled for a simple and unfulfilling life. I still believe that the Lord is performing great and miraculous things for those that believe. I often think about the time I was in the hospital with little hope of living. I was in such pain that I almost gave up on life. My wife and sons were very concerned about my health and even living. One of my sons (Eric) declared while I was suffering in the hospital to believe that the Lord God would not give up on me and I would live. That was over ten years ago! My faith increased at the Word of God given by my son and days later I was released from the hospital. I learned a valuable spiritual lesson those times I was in the hospital with severe sickness. I learned to believe and hear what the Lord is saying to me. What is the Lord saying to His people about His return and taking His people to glory?

When I read *Revelation 3:14-22*, the Lord Jesus expresses the nature of the lukewarm church. If we read in detail the nature of this church, we will find that it had little regard for the coming of the Lord. They were neither cold nor hot; not on fire for the Lord nor ice cold. What does this mean? They were not excited about the Lord's return nor totally unbelieving. The Lord said that because they were neither cold nor hot, He would vomit them out of His mouth. I believe if the church remains in a lukewarm state, we will not see the glory of the Lord in our lives nor maybe being caught up to meet the Lord in the air. There are different interpretations of the Laodicean church. Some interpret this as the church just before the Coming of the Lord. Chapter four of *Revelation (NKJV)* begins: *"After these things I looked, and behold, a door standing open in heaven. And the first voice which I heard was like a trumpet speaking with me, saying, "Come up here, and I will show you things which must take place after this."* Some Bible scholars believe that the Laodicean church is the last stage of the church before the coming of the Lord Jesus to earth to receive His church. This may be a controversial topic among different church denominations. However, after careful study from different Biblical scholars I am convinced that this revelation is true. Please remember, this is not my own interpretation but careful study of Bible scholars that believed and have given serious study to the coming of the Lord. Regardless of what we may believe of what man's interpretation may be, we rely on the written Word for clarification. The Word of the Lord declares that Jesus is coming back for a church; *"that He (Jesus) might sanctify and cleanse her with the washing of water by the word, that He might present her to Himself a glorious church, not having spot or wrinkle or any such thing, but that she (the church) should be holy and without blemish." (Ephesians 5:26-27, NKJV).* That's the real meaning for us to be ready and stay ready!

We can explain the Coming of the Lord and all the details that are associated with the glorious revelation of the Coming of the Lord. The most important consideration is will you be ready when Jesus comes? One of the crude aspects of the Lord's coming and His church being caught up into Heaven is the great unbelief of saints and sinners. The longer we wait it seems as though the greater people are falling away from believing that the Lord is coming. Let us take a serious look at what is happening in our world. On **May**

14, 1948, David Ben-Gurion, the head of the Jewish Agency, proclaimed the establishment of the State of Israel with U.S. President Harry S. Truman recognizing the new nation on the same day. The establishment of the State of Israel became a major milestone for Israel and the rest of the world. However, it is very important that we are very familiar with the scriptures, so we do not allow any mistakes in our interpretation of the scriptures. Consider *Matthew 24:14, NKJV: "And this gospel of the kingdom will be preached in all the world as a witness to all the nations, and then the end will come."* In *Matthew 24:3*, the disciples ask Jesus, the sign of His coming, and the end of the age. *Matthew 24:14* gives the answer to this question. Consider these actions that the Lord Jesus told His disciples in *Matthew 24:4-14, NKJV):*

1. *Many will come in the name of Christ and deceive many.*
2. *You will hear of wars and rumors of wars.*
3. *Nation will rise against nation, and kingdom against kingdom.*
4. *There will be famines, pestilences, and earthquakes in various places.*
5. *You will be delivered up for tribulation and you will be killed.*
6. *You will be hated by all nations for My name's sake.*

7. *Many will be offended, will betray one another, and will hate one another.*

8. *Many false prophets will rise and deceive many.*

9. *Lawlessness will abound, and the love of many will grow cold.*

10. *The Gospel of the Kingdom will be preached in all the world as a witness to all the nations, and then the end will come.*

The ten points that I have noted from the scriptures should be carefully considered as a basic thesis to the understanding of the coming of the Lord Jesus Christ. We are not given the day nor the hour when the Lord Jesus returns. *(Matthew 24:36-44; Mark 13:32-33; Luke 21:34-36).* However, we are given the strength and power to live holy and be ready to go back with Jesus when He returns to receive His church. Our job is to be ready based on the life we should live towards Almighty God and one another. Many people think that our lives towards Almighty God and others is too difficult. This is why the Lord filled us with His Holy Spirit *(Acts 2:38-39)* so that we can learn of His holiness and be ready when He returns to earth to receive His church. Think about this; why would the Lord come to earth, die on a cross, be buried in a grave, and rise from the dead after three days and three nights? After Jesus' resurrection from the dead and accession into Heaven,

He sent back the Holy Spirit to all that were willing to receive it to be witnesses throughout the earth. All this was done that we might have the right to the Tree of Life. Everything that the Lord did was in love. The Lord cares for us and wills that all be saved and come to the knowledge of the truth *(1 Timothy 2:4).* Almighty God wants us to be prepared for His coming. He does not want the man that He made and love to die and miss Heaven. We must think about the mercy of our Lord for all mankind. Throughout history the sinfulness of mankind was beyond measure. When we read the scriptures our hearts tremble at the wicked things that mankind did to others and their disregard for Almighty God. Nevertheless, it did not matter how far the extent of violence and wickedness that took place among mankind. Almighty God loved His people and made a way for us to escape the evil that had come upon us. I do not think I can over emphasize the meaning of Jesus' sacrifice to free us from the sin that had us spiritually bound and awaiting the kingdom of darkness. The Lord God knew we could not deliver ourselves, nor the constant natural sacrifices and offerings that would free us from the constant sin that entered our lives. Human beings needed full deliverance that could only be given by the Mediator between God and man, Jesus Christ! When we read about the sinful struggles that mankind had throughout their lifetime, we were at the point of giving up. The level of difficulty to please Almighty

God was beyond the power that existed within us. We needed a Savior that would deliver us from the sin that had us bound.

I am grateful to our Lord Jesus Christ for the victory we have through His broken body and shed blood. Without His broken body and shed blood there would be no remission of sins. We are free today from the awful plague of sin that overshadowed our lives. We are no longer slaves to sin! We have been delivered from the unrighteous acts of sin and the awful plague of sin that destroys our lives. The Word of the Lord declares: *"For if we have been united together in the likeness of His death, certainly we also shall be in the likeness of His resurrection, knowing this, that our old man was crucified with Him, that the body of sin might be done away with, that we should no longer be slaves of sin." (Romans 6:5-6, NKJV)*. If we consider *Romans 6:5-6*, we will understand that we have been united with Christ and with our brothers and sisters, through the likeness of Christ's death and resurrection. The scriptures *(Romans 6:4 and Colossians 2:12)* declares that we are buried with Him in baptism which is the likeness of His death, and we are raised with Christ through faith, which is the likeness of His resurrection! Just imagine if there was no physical work by mankind that could have moved Almighty God to save us from our sins. However, it was faith in our Lord Jesus Christ and the magnificent work that was done at Calvary that brought us to salvation and is keeping us unto this present hour. It is important that we never forget that our salvation is incorporated in the death, burial, and resurrection of our Lord Jesus Christ! There is no plan other than the plan of salvation that can cleanse us from unrighteousness except the Blood of Jesus Christ! Salvation is only through Jesus Christ our Lord. Let us accept the Word of the Lord and live abundantly in Christ Jesus. Our lives will be changed, and we will have that blessed hope of the Lord's coming which is the greatest spiritual event that mankind will ever achieve! Will you be ready to go back with Jesus when He comes?

Fifteen

SONGS OF FAITH AND HEAVENLY EXPECTATION

Oh, I want to see Him, look upon His face,
There to sing forever of His saving grace;
On the streets of glory let me lift my voice,
Cares all past, home at last, ever to rejoice.

The song, *"Oh I Want To See Him"* was written in 1916 after the Azusa Street Revival. The **Azusa Street Revival** was a historic revival meeting that took place in Los Angeles, California. It was led by William J. Seymour, an African-American preacher. The start of the three-year revival began on April 9,1906 and continued until roughly until 1915. Many songs and sermons were written and produced during the Azusa Revival. Most of the songs were handed down through churches via choirs and sermons. The basic message of these songs and sermons was the Coming of the Lord. If you study the meaning of these songs and sermons, you will find that there was a great emphasis on the return of the Lord Jesus to earth to take His people to glory. The Apostolic Pentecostal churches were one of the major advocates announcing the return of the Lord Jesus to earth. Many songs were written to encourage the children of Almighty God to fight the good fight of faith and hold on until the Coming of the Lord. The saints of the Lord God, during that time had a high expectation for the return of the Lord. Regardless of their financial condition, they eected their lives would change for the best when Jesus returned to receive His church into glory. Many people thought that the Lord would come any day. Therefore, they made sure that they were ready to go back with Jesus when He returned. Their expectation of the Lord's return gave them a reason to live holy and see the Lord. Times were not so easy for people in the early 1900's, especially for African Americans. Nevertheless, the church was a great center of hope and assurance for most people that believed in Christ Jesus. Many believers waited with great expectancy for the return of the Lord Jesus because of the dire conditions in the earth. When the saints of God gathered in churches and homes, there was great anticipation for the Jesus' return. Many songs gave hope to the children of Almighty God of a new day, and a day without struggle and hardship. The people of God came to church often, sometimes four days or more a week, with the expectation of the Lord' return at any time. Great sermons were preached, and wonderful songs were created to elevate the faith of the children of Almighty God. Regardless of the financial conditions of the saints they served the Lord Jesus gratefully and with great expectation of His return. Everything that was learned from the scriptures gave the people of Almighty God hope that one day Jesus would return and take them to glory. These and many other songs about the coming of the Lord also gave the people of God a desire to continue in the faith until the Lord Jesus returned.

I pray that every child of Almighty God will find strength in the Word of the Lord that they may continue to keep holding on to the Lord's unchanging hand. The Gospel world has changed so much since the times when churches held high standards of holiness. It does not mean that that the Lord has forgotten us or tossed us aside. The Lord still loves us and is willing to speak to our hearts to bring us back into His lovingkindness. Remember the scripture; *"For this is good and acceptable in the sight of God our Savior, who desires all men to be saved and to come to the knowledge of the truth." (1 Timothy 2:3-4, NKJV).* Even in our worse sinful condition, the Lord God does not desire that we perish because of the sinfulness that may have overtaken our lives. The Lord is here to deliver us from whatever state of unrighteousness we may be in. All we must do is submit ourselves to the Lord and ask Him to help and guide us to victory.

During the latter part of the seventies through the nineties, Walter Hawkins and Tramaine Hawkins composed and sang a very popular song entitled, "Goin' Up Yonder." Consider the lyrics:

Goin' Up Yonder
By Walter Hawkins & Tramaine Hawkins

I'm goin' up yonder
I'm goin' up yonder
I'm goin' up yonder
To be with my Lord

Goin' Up Yonder moved the hearts of many young saints. It had the rhythmic style that appealed to young people yet sending a powerful message about the Lord's return to earth and taking His people to glory. The song has the movement of modern-day R & B, yet a profound message about living for Jesus and going back to heaven when He comes. This is the hope of every born-again believer; to live with Christ and go back with Him when He returns. This song expresses the hope of every born-again believer. The more we live on this earth the more we realize that evil continues to get worse. If we read the scriptures as found in *(2 Timothy 3:1-9)*, we conclude that the sinful nature of this world is not getting better but getting worse and will soon lead to ultimate corruption. Nevertheless, when we read the scriptures, pray, and have blessed communion with the children of God, our focus is redirected. We do not concentrate so much on the things of the world but on the things of Heaven.

Music has always been a smoothing relief for the mind. Remember when David played the harp to refresh the evil spirit that troubled Saul *(1 Samuel 16:22-23)*? The music that David played refreshed the spirit of Saul that gave him peace and calm during his troubled times. If we carefully read the Bible, we will find that music played an important factor in the lives of the children of God during the times of trouble and war. Let us consider one examples: When Judah was confronted by the armies of Ammon, Moab, and Mount Seir, King Jehoshaphat was informed by the Lord that the battle was not his but the Lord's! Read the scriptures before and after *(2 Chronicles 20:20)* that helped King Jehoshaphat win the battle. The battle was not won by conventional means of war, but it was the Word of the Lord that instructed King Jehoshaphat to send the praises out first. The strategy that was given by the Lord allowed King Jehoshaphat of Judah and the inhabitants of Jerusalem to overcome their enemies without fighting and getting hurt. Children of Almighty God should listen to the Lord very carefully as we engage in the attacks rendered by the devil. We never know the strategy that the Lord will give us to overcome the devil. Remember the song by Yolanda Adams, *"The Battle Is The Lord's."*

Let's consider another song:

Will You Be Ready
By Commissioned

Let's all make a stand, stand up for what
you know is right
Most importantly, Keep the love of Jesus
always on your mind
And you've gotta be ready
(You don't wanna be left out here after
Jesus is gone)
Be ready when Jesus comes

King Hezekiah king of Judah was threatened by Sennacherib king of Assyria. King Hezekiah and Judah did not have the military might to defend itself against Sennacherib and the Assyrians. However, Hezekiah took the letter he had received from the Assyrians and spread it before the Lord and prayed. Hezekiah understood that his only hope was in the Lord. Judah was not able to defend itself against the power of the Assyrians. His only line of defense was to depend on the Lord God to fight for them. Therefore, Hezekiah prayed before the Lord God and concluded his prayer in this manner: *"Now therefore, O LORD our God, I pray,* *save us from his hand, that all the kingdoms of the earth may know that You are the LORD God, You alone." (2 Kings 19:19, NKJV).* When we read the scriptures, we find that King Hezekiah and Judah did not need to fight against King Sennacherib and the Assyria army. Note the scripture: *"And it came to pass on a certain night that the angel of the LORD went out, and killed in the camp of the Assyrians one hundred and eighty-five thousand;" (2 Kings 19:35a, NKJV).* The Lord God fought for Hezekiah and Judah and defeated the Assyrians. I believe the Lord God will fight for us when opposition comes against us. Hezekiah was ready because the Lord made him and all of Judah understand that He (The Lord) would fight for them. I believe the Lord will make us ready during our everyday walk in Christ so we will be prepared to go back with the Lord when He comes. I am convinced the Lord has given His people the power to overcome every obstacle and problem that tries to pull us away from our salvation. Our hope in Christ Jesus is to keep fighting and keep winning that we may go back with Jesus when He returns. Oh, what a day that will be! There will be great freedom and glory that cannot be expressed in human terms. We will live with Jesus for all eternity in the blessedness and glory that cannot be imagined! As the song declares, *"Will You Be Ready When Jesus Comes?"*

References

Adams, Yolanda; *"The Battle Is The Lord's."* Save The World, 1993, Genre: Christian/Gospel

Azusa Street Revival: *"Oh I Want To See Him"* Written in 1916 after the Azusa Street Revival. The **Azusa Street Revival**; Los Angeles, CA. Led by William J. Seymour, an African-American preacher. The three-year revival began on April 9,1906 and continued until roughly until 1915.

Batzig, Nicholas T., Old Testament Personal Types and Shadows of Christ; Christian Apologetics & Intelligence Ministry

Commissioned; "Will You Be Ready?" Lyrics edit by from the album; Will You Be Ready by Commissioned; from the album Will You Be Ready

Cornelius, Rufus H., Oh, I Want to See Him, 1916; *copyright status is Public Domain* Subject: Anticipation; Scripture: 1 John 3:2

Franklin, Benjamin (1706-1790); *"If you fail to plan, you are planning to fail!"* Quotable Quotes; a writer, a philosopher, a scientist, a politician, a patriot, a Founding Father, an inventor, and publisher. He helped with the founding of the United States of America

Hawkins, Walter; Goin' Up Yonder (1975) Artist: The Love Center Choir; Album: The Light Years, Released: 1994; Genre: Easy listening

Knigh, Marie; I'm Going To Work Until The Day Is Done" (1975)

Newton, John; Amazing Grace" is a Christian hymn published in 1779, with words written in 1772 by the English poet and Anglican clergyman John Newton (1725–1807)

Oatman, Jr. Johnson; Count Your Blessings; pub. 1897; *copyright status, public domain* Subject: Thanksgiving, Praise; Scripture: Psalm 40:5; 1 Thessalonians 5:18; Ephesians 1:3; Edwin O. Excell

Spurgeon, Charles, The Blood of Abel, and the Blood of Jesus, September 2, 1866, Scripture: Genesis 4:10; Hebrews 12:24 From: Metropolitan Tabernacle Pulpit Volume 12

Behold, I tell you a mystery: We shall not all sleep, but we shall all be changed— in a moment, in the twinkling of an eye, at the last trumpet. For the trumpet will sound, and the dead will be raised incorruptible, and we shall be changed. (1 Corinthians 15:51-52, NKJV).

Printed in the United States
by Baker & Taylor Publisher Services